P E T E R I

VIRTUAL POWER TEAMS

How to Deliver Projects Faster, Reduce Costs,
and Develop Your Organization
for the Future!

CASTLE MOUNT MEDIA GMBH & CO. KG
Burgbergstr. 94c
91054 Erlangen
Germany
www.castlemountmedia.com

Bibliographic Information from the German National Library
can be found under http://dnb.d-nb.de

Printed in the United States of America and for International
Distribution in the United Kingdom

Book design by Susan Veach

Translation by Laura Baxter

ISBN 978-3-9818472-3-9 (Paperback)
ISBN 978-3-9818472-4-6 (eBook)

Table of Contents

An Earthquake Shakes Things Up 7

PART I – CLARITY
1. The Greater the Distance Between Team Members, the More Imperative it is to know Your Colleagues Personally 15
2. Bringing Together a Great Team Leads to a Phenomenal Success 43
3. It is Easy to Lead When Everyone has a Goal and is Allowed to Shine 59
4. When Goals are Interlinked, Each Team Member is Accountable 77
5. When Team Roles Meet the True Strengths of the Team Member, Work is Pleasing 93

PART II – COMMUNICATION
6. How Technology Helps Bridge Continents and Time Zones 111
7. Structured Communication Means that not only the Boss talks, but Everyone Talks - about Everything 131
8. Structure and Processes Create the Basis – Trust Unlocks the Team's Power 149

PART III – Culture
9. Virtual Power Teams Can Quickly React to Changes and Take Advantage of Opportunities and Trends 169
10. Whoever Promotes Diversity instead of Combating It, Raises Potential 181
11. Extraordinary Achievements Deserve Extraordinary Rewards – for Everyone 203
12. When a Virtual Power Team Splits Apart, a New Team is Quickly Born 215

Epilogue 223
The Author 233

In this book, I tell a story which shows what is possible with virtual power teams. The story and the people involved are imaginary. Parallels to real situations, however, is absolutely intentional. My story begins with a shocking occurrence.

A few weeks after I wrote about this fictional event, I, myself, was shocked: A very similar occurrence happened in the same region as in my book. Shocking, dreadful pictures were spread around the world.

I never would have thought that such a thing could happen. For a long time, I considered changing my story, because reality seemed to be taking over. After long contemplation, I decided to indeed publish my original story. The story at the beginning of the book is, unfortunately, very realistic. Perhaps the solutions that are presented in this book will also one day become a reality. That would truly be a reason to celebrate.

An Earthquake Shakes Things Up

The iPad alarm brought Bernd out of a deep sleep. It was half-past-six in the morning. The entrepreneur stirred reluctantly in bed. His eyelids were heavy. He wanted to keep on sleeping. His aching body reminded him of yesterday's late-night training at the gym. Even-so, thoughts about the news day were racing through his head: Frankfurt! Another project delay, but somehow the foundations must be finished this month. Why hadn't the construction manager called back? What are today's appointments? Who will pick up Lena from the airport tonight?

At the thought of his daughter's arrival he sat straight up in bed. Lena. Airport. Moving drowsily, he took the iPad off the night table and opened his e-mail. Suddenly breaking new appeared:

Earthquake at the foot of the Himalayas - thousands homeless in Transmontania

Instantly, Bernd was wide awake. The Google Alert notifications, set to immediately inform him of any natural catastrophes, had his full attention. As a former company consultant, Bernd is specialized in the organization of construction and infrastructure projects, and he wants to expand his business internationally. If he were to participate in the reconstruction after this disaster, he could help those afflicted on – where is it again? – Transmontania. This was the chance he had been looking for.

Over the years Bernd's vision for his company has changed and developed. Initially, he had been consulting companies in how to save costs and maximize profits. Today this was no longer enough for him. He wanted his work to make the world a better place. Could this be his chance?

He was shocked. It was just half-past nine in the Himalayas, and the first images of the disaster were appearing on Twitter. Bernd saw people crying in front of collapsed houses with the mighty Himalayas rising in the background behind them. He had never heard of Transmontania. Reading the first reports, he learned the remote region had recently declared its independence. Yet, in a few short hours, 80 percent of the local homes had been destroyed.

Fortunately, minor shocks had announced the impending earthquake, and when the first houses started collapsing many inhabitants had already fled. But now, thousands were homeless.

The pictures of the Earthquake are terrible, but this is the opportunity Bernd has been waiting for: He wants to build earthquake-proof houses for a whole country.

Bernd looked more closely at the photos on Twitter. His professional eye saw how primitively the one- and two-story houses were built, and how unstable they were. If they rebuild them the same way, he thought, they'll just collapse again in the next earthquake. These people needed different houses. Modern houses. Earthquake-proof houses.

This was it, the chance he had been waiting for. By now he had a lot of experience with construction projects in Germany, and he had a vision: earthquake-proof houses for Transmontania. But how would he get such a project? Who would design the new houses? Who would construct them? And how would the locals afford the houses? The region seemed to be poor.

He got up, went into the kitchen, poured water into the espresso machine, and pressed the button for a lungo. His mind shifted to his friend Claude as the machine hummed along. Espresso! Claude's favorite drink. Claude, a young architect from Montreal, drank espresso hourly, except when he slept. Claude would have an idea, most certainly! The successful Canadian had already created complete residential areas and worked with teams of architects from all over the world. And Claude loved collaborating over the Internet. His latest project for Montreal was a large public building which he had designed with a team of colleagues from across four continents.

"I need to talk to Claude as soon as possible," Bernd said to himself. He sent him a greeting through Skype's messenger and asked for a quick chat. Then he sat down at the kitchen table with his coffee and his iPad. Through the window he could see a cloudy and rainy Hamburg, but his thoughts were at the foot of the Himalayas. What is the latest on Google News or Twitter?

The capital of Transmontania seemed largely unaffected by the earthquake. The infrastructure was still intact. The government sent out an international call for help via the Internet. On their own, the government would not be able to help the homeless in the remote rural earthquake areas. Any assistance would be welcome: food, clothing, money or technical support. They were hoping that there weren't too many buried or injured people, but so far they were unable to confirm the situation.

Claude, the young architect from Canada, will be able to help Bernd. He has worked with teams from all over the world.

Bernd went to the Transmontania government website, where he fortunately found an English translation. On the home page he saw that a young female official named Anne Tan had just been appointed Aid Management Coordinator for the earthquake catastrophe. An e-mail address was also provided. Bernd began writing a note to offer his help.

Claude sent over a message over Skype: "Hi, I'm coming in straight from dinner with friends on Rue Saint-Denis. Do you still wanna talk?" (It was just before midnight over in Montreal.)

"Yes, that would be great," Bernd answered.

Global Cooperation - The Great Challenge of Our Time

According to Forrester Research, 81% of the workforce in industrialized countries regularly works with people who are not in the same location. Instead they work in their own home, in another city, or even on the other side of the world. Additionally, 60% of all teams consist of members with different ethnic or cultural backgrounds. All of this occurs at a time when all worldly knowledge doubles every two years. According to some estimates, this doubling of knowledge will soon occur every six months. People work together over vast distances and they bring different cultural, social, linguistic and personal characteristics into their work place. They also deal with an ever-increasing flood of new information. A gigantic challenge! And that's not all. In addition, there are the problems that arise which affect large numbers of the population, such as natural disasters, which may be the result of climate change and an ever-increasing world population, an increase in regional wars and the related flows of refugees, the problematic dependence of the economy on the scarcity of oil, a fragile global financial system, and the vulnerability of our new high-tech infrastructures.

Challenges of the future will require expertise and excellence. Virtual teams will help you find the experts you need to successfully reach your goals.

The new world in which we live needs new forms of cooperation. It needs diverse groups from different cultures who are able to overcome geographic and cultural boundaries and to meet the challenges of a new era. Such teams are now needed everywhere: in companies, among the self-employed and freelancers, in non-governmental organizations (NGOs) and in politics. The question is how can these teams provide optimal performance under such circumstances? Without top notch performance, we have no chance to meet the challenges of the future. The problems are too great to cope with half-way.

Unfortunately, so-called "virtual teams," where people work together across geographical distances, are often seen as the unfortunate but necessary consequence of globalization. These virtual teams, however, offer us a huge opportunity -- especially when they cross not only geographical but also cultural boundaries. These geographical and cultural differences are exactly the factor that gives virtual teams their strength. When you seize the opportunity to incorporate the virtual teams into your organization, and you understand how to use these strengths to your advantage, your virtual teams become virtual power teams. Virtual power teams are the teams of the future! They are the teams of innovation and will not only solve global problems but also recognize and seize economic opportunities. They will create new prosperity not only for a few, but for many. This is how the potential of a connected and united world unfolds.

Where there is a Worthy Goal, there are Worthy Employees... *Worldwide*

The younger generation would rather work on exciting projects than to pursue a classic career in a traditional, hierarchical organization. They are already accustomed to communicating and engaging globally within university systems and international communities. For them, it is more important to know the characteristics of the organization in which they work. They want to understand the impact it makes, the traces it leaves, and whether or not it makes the world a better place. There are a lot of people, especially younger ones, who work globally and want to contribute to projects around the world.

On the other hand, there are entrepreneurs and managers in existing organizations that also need these younger people in order to achieve their new and ambitious goals.

In virtual teams, it is important to create and maintain a gravitational force around your energy core: your common goal. This allows each team member to be free to shine – to be a star.

Nowadays, it is possible to start new projects -- or even whole businesses -- completely virtually. Entrepreneurs, freelancers, managers in companies, or activists in NGOs can find and mobilize the best employees anywhere in the world. The challenge is to enable these teams by giving them the power and strength they need despite the geographical distance or cultural differences. A virtual team is built like an atom. At its center is the nucleus, the core of the atom, and it has various particles orbiting around it. Gravity attracts and holds the particles in their orbits. In your virtual team, like in the atom, there has to be a gravitational pull that holds your team together despite the geographical distance between the members. This gravity which pulls the team members together is the team's purpose and goal. It is what inspires and motivates all members to achieve a higher performance. Each member of the team is attracted to and held by this core.

In poorly managed virtual teams, the gravitational force is lost over time. The individual particles move further and further away from the core until they fall out of orbit. Virtual power teams have not only a strong core and a constant gravitational force, but they also become stronger rather than weaker over time. What it takes for virtual teams to become virtual power teams is explained in the next few chapters of this book.

With virtual power teams, organizations can be globally present and have access to global resources. They are more flexible, scalable and have a much greater source of information and knowledge.

The prerequisites to create strong virtual power teams have never been as prevalent and available as they are today. Numerous digital platforms, such as LinkedIn or Fiverr, open the door to a giant world-wide expert pool at the click of a mouse. Every entrepreneur, every executive, and every member of an NGO can now acquire the best specialists in the world on predication that a strong bond between individual experts can be achieved. Furthermore, this bond is strengthened by the desire to work towards a common goal, which, in turn, creates a powerful, ambitious spirit. This will help bridge the geographical and cultural differences of the team members.

Running a virtual team means unrivaled responsibility. In local teams, the human presence ensures that the team members support and inspire each other. In virtual teams, the leadership must create an effective team culture to ensure that the geographical and emotional distances are bridged. The leadership of a virtual team is, therefore, primarily leadership of people. The leaders of the future do not require rank and status, but require special communication skills in dealing with and uniting people from varied backgrounds.

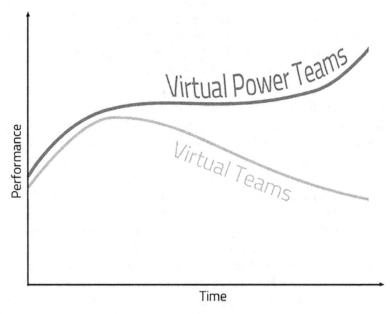

Illustration 1: Virtual Power Teams

Virtual power teams use three groups equally: the responsible leaders, the individual team members, and, finally, the entire organization. For executives, the advantage is that they have a selection of top employees from all over the world with whom they can achieve outstanding results. The individual team members can participate in exciting international projects without having to constantly travel. This gives them the opportunity to develop their professional skills and take on increasingly challenging tasks, while having more time and flexibility to do things they would like to do and to be with those people who are important to them, their friends and family. The entire organization - whether it is a group, medium-sized company, scientific institution or NGO - can be globally present, and it has access to global resources. It is flexible, scalable and can use existing knowledge instead of having to invest in individual training. When a series of virtual power teams achieve top results, the entire organization will eventually be among the best.

Do you want to be among the winners of a new era? Then read on and follow the story of Bernd from Hamburg, and his worldwide virtual power team. Learn how to create a strong bond between top experts across geographical and cultural boundaries, and create a passion for achieving high goals. Benefit from the experience of the pioneers of virtual power teams, who share these with you in exclusive interviews and in an exciting virtual conversation. Enjoy!

PART 1

CLARITY

Chapter 1

The Greater the Distance Between Team Members, the More Imperative It Is to Know Your Colleagues Personally

Bernd has been sitting in his bathrobe at the kitchen table for twenty minutes. His e-mail to the coordinator for earthquake relief in Transmontania has been written, and the cup of coffee next to him has gotten cold. All of his thoughts were devoted to the construction of the earthquake-proof houses in the Himalayas. As yet he had no plan, but he reasoned: the contract first - then the plan. This was an iterative approach. Or was it arrogance? Carefully, he listed his references: several successful multimillion euro construction projects that he had coordinated in Germany. So far, he had made every appointment and kept every budget. He was proud of that. With the Asians I can do it even better, thought Bernd. They are so reliable. It's important that his e-mail sound confident even if his English was sometimes awkward and not always free from errors. He envied Claude, who changed between French, English, Spanish, Russian, and Italian, as other people change between radio stations.

Bernd writes an email to Anne, the Coordinator for earthquake relief in Transmontania. He wants to have the construction order, and then make a plan.

At the same moment, he saw the architect's smiling face on his iPad; Claude was calling again via Skype. Bernd tapped the green button to answer the conversation and saw a video of Claude in his apartment on the plateau, the most fashionable city district of Montreal. The young Canadian wore a casual cut light gray suit and a black shirt.

"Dude, how are you? Wow, no need to dress up for the occasion," Claude joked about Bernd's bathrobe, and then grinned. Bernd was tempted to switch off the Skype video quickly, but he did not want to be the humorless German.

"Hey, it's six o'clock in the morning, as if you didn't know," Bernd replied sarcastically. "There's something serious I would like to talk to you about. Have you heard about the earthquake in Asia?"

"Yeah, I saw it on CNN when I came in," Claude answered. "Terrible. Fortunately, it seems that no lives have been lost, but the houses are all scrap. Why do you ask? Are you thinking about doing something?"

"Well, they really need someone to rebuild their houses, and the houses should be built in such a way that they are able to survive any further earthquakes. What do you think?" Bernd asked.

"Well, you own a well-oiled German construction machine, but have you ever done projects on other continents?"

"We had international teams on the company's advisory board," Bernd thought out loud, "but I've never managed projects with global teams myself. That is what worries me a little. As you know, I don't like surprises. Fortunately, I know you! So, tell me, how do you manage to work in Canada, and yet your team is working all over the world?"

"In different ways," Claude explained." For example, on the project in Pakistan, I was actually here in Canada, and the other team members were in other countries. This worked because we made the complete design over an MOOC. Actually, with an MOOC, you could collaboratively create a new

Claude proposes a MOOC (Massive Open Online Course) for the house design. Sometimes tens of thousands of people are involved in the project over the Internet.

earthquake-resistant house design for Transmontania. You will probably not make people happy with German architecture, right? So it would be important to consider local building traditions. The materials you use should be sustainable and come from the region. Best of all, the locals themselves should build their new houses. Otherwise at the end only Western companies earn from the deal - and Transmontania drowns in debt."

"I feel the same way. But please, what is a moock or whatever it's called?" asked Bernd.

"'MOOC' stands for Massive Open Online Course. In these virtual university courses, tens of thousands of students learn together over the Internet. The best thing is that they usually work on projects for a short six weeks! In Pakistan, we had 25,000 students who submitted 5000 designs for a proposed building! Many students were very advanced, so the quality of the proposals was outstanding. We then built one of the designs from that MOOC on behalf of the Pakistani government."

"How much did it cost? "

"In our case, nothing at all, because the U.S. professor who had organized the MOOC gave the draft to the Pakistani government."

Bernd began, "We could certainly do the same for Transmontania. After all, people urgently need help. It just concerns me to think that I should manage 25,000 students and monitor their progress."

"Manage 25,000 students?" asked Claude. "That's not possible. You're thinking in old world ways. In the networked virtual world, you will not get anywhere with micromanagement and control. Give people what they need - and then leave them alone."

"Micromanaging in the networked, virtual world will hold you back and weaken your team," Claude explained to Bernd. Can Bernd let go of his old habits?

"Claude," Bernd asked firmly. "Are you going to be part of this adventure? Will you help me organize the workflow of designing the new houses?"

"You know," Claude answered with a calm tone, "I have two weaknesses: one for people in need, and one for old friends like you. I'm with you! But only for one day a week! I don't have more time than that to give."

"Thank you! As a first step, I'll try to reach the Government Commissioner in Transmontania by e-mail and arrange a Skype conference with her. I'm going to invite you to it also. Okay? You know how I hate telephone conferences ..."

Bernd finished the conversation with Claude and sent the e-mail to Anne Tan. He then took a shower, got dressed, and said goodbye to his wife, who had just gotten up. He drove to his office in the harbor district, and spent the rest of the day tracking current projects in Germany. He telephoned and answered e-mails until Noon. He then went to Bremen and visited a construction site. Afterwards, he drove to the airport to pick up his daughter who arrived late that evening. At age 14, Lena was returning home from her first school class trip abroad.

Three days later, Bernd sat in his office preparing to lead his first international telephone conference. The spring sun was shining through the large windows and brightly illuminating his workspace. Bernd really wanted to do this project. He was still affected by the pictures from Transmontania - but he also urgently needed new projects. The German market had not developed as much as he had hoped. In addition, an important customer had declared bankruptcy just two weeks ago. It was high time to do business internationally. If only this new technology was not so annoying! Bernd liked to have close personal contact with all project participants. He traveled by car, train, or plane every week, and telephoned several hours a day. Skype, FaceTime, WhatsApp and all these other programs were unpleasant. But he knew he would have to get used to the virtual world now.

Luckily, Claude was there. He always knew the latest technology, and video conferencing and virtual collaboration were part of everyday life for the young Canadian. If anything goes wrong, Claude will help me, thought Bernd.

The first Skype conference with Claude and Anne is an unusual challenge for Bernd. He thinks he's well-prepared for it, though.

It was now just before three in the afternoon, and the conference was about to start. Bernd went his over his agenda again:

1. Scope, timeframe, and budget of the project
2. Construction of sustainable, earthquake-proof houses
3. Possibilities of financing

Bernd looked at the user interface of Skype again. Always these automatic updates! No sooner do you learn where the buttons are, when everything looks different again.

At precisely 3 pm, Bernd saw the photos of Claude and Anne, the young government employee from Transmontania, appear on the screen. Claude initiated contact first:

"Hi, it's seven o'clock in the morning in Montreal. I'm still lying in bed! Better leave the live picture frame off, or you'll be envious of my cool sheets."

"OK," said Bernd tensely. For a moment, he was disappointed that Claude was apparently so casual in participating in this important telephone conference. Then the young Asian woman joined in.

"Good evening, gentlemen. Or good morning, depending on the time in your location. This is Anne Tan."

"May I call you Anne?" Claude replied. "I am Claude. Anne sounds pretty ... European, isn't it? "

"Hello, Claude! My mother is English, and I studied in Cambridge."

"Maybe I could ..." Bernd said.

"Oh, sorry, Bernd, I'm so terribly sorry," Claude said with much excitement. "You are leading the conference, of course! I'm going to be quiet now – unless you need me to say something."

Anne interrupts the conference and seems to be talking to a child. Claude is still in bed. For Bernd, everything seems unfamiliar.

Bernd introduced both Claude and Anne to his agenda, then gave Anne the floor. She spoke slowly, with well-chosen words. To Bernd she sounded like a government spokesperson on Downing Street. Anne explained that the Transmontanian government had already prepared an announcement for the rebuilding of the houses. Time was of the essence, since everything had to be finished before the winter to avoid another catastrophe. During the summer months, they could relocate the people to tents, but that was untenable in winter. The World Bank would probably compensate for the material costs and the wages of the local workers, but they were uncertain about the remaining funding. Project management, drafts, and international employees had to be viewed separately. The Prime Minister was fond of Bernd's idea to rebuild the houses in an earthquake-proof manner. But if it were not possible to finance it, they would have to resort to traditional methods of home building. Nothing had been decided yet. While she was talking, the voice of a child could be heard in the background. At one point Anne paused shortly and seemed to be speaking to the child. Her words sounded kind and friendly -- almost as if she were singing.

Bernd thought to himself: What a challenge! He was still a little nervous. He wasn't used to any of this: the project management, the hope for suitable drafts from some people around the world, and the open question about financing. But he was determined to go on: this would be his international breakthrough. Besides, he could not get the images of distraught people standing in rubble in front of their

Anne wants to get a specialist from London to lead the crowdfunding. Bernd, on the other hand, says he is the boss and should take care of himself.

destroyed homes out of his head. Bernd would let Claude organize the MOOC thing. For a German businessman like him, all of this sounded risky, but Bernd was ready to try new things. Claude also wanted to manage financing via crowdfunding. Should Bernd agree to this?

"About the financing via crowdfunding," said Bernd into the microphone. "I'm not that experienced with it yet and have also read a couple of negative reports about it. Please give me a week to get informed, then we'll see."

"Well, Bernd," Claude interrupted. "With all due respect – now you really are forcing me to interrupt you-- I think we should get an expert on crowdfunding into the team a.s.a.p., define the parameters and let the expert get started."

"I think so, too," Anne agreed. "Through my contacts in London I have access to top specialists in the field of new methods of financing. I have already been able to finance agricultural development projects in distant mountain regions this way. I'll make proposals for the parameters and send you a list with possible contacts tomorrow evening our time at the latest."

"Thank you for the offer," Bernd responded. "But I should take care of this. I will deal with this in the next few days. As soon as I know more, I will send you an e-mail and we can arrange the next conference appointment to make a final decision on the parameters and the financing."

Claude accuses Bernd of creating obstacle through micromanaging. He recommends that Bernd work with a mentor. Bernd, however, believes that he does not need a coach.

Bernd ended the teleconference with some words of thanks and good wishes. His agenda was finished, and yet, he felt uncomfortable. On the one hand, Anne was likeable to him. She seemed confident, perfectly educated, linked up internationally, and a quick thinker. But financing was really *his* task as the initiator of the project! He wasn't used to others being ahead of him when he was the boss. Several times during the call, he felt as if the other two knew more than he did, and he didn't like that one bit.

Another Skype call came in – it was Claude. Bernd pressed the green button with slight irritation.

"Are you crazy? What kind of statement was that?" Claude seemed really upset. And Bernd didn't know the smart young architect that well. "How can you be this dominant and thwart people who want to take over a task? *'Thanks for the offer but I should take care of this.'* Man! You can't lead a virtual team like this -- at least not if you want to keep adhering to deadlines. Whenever your team members are excited and want to contribute their expertise, you should encourage them and just let them do it."

"How do I know I can trust Anne?" Bernd asked. "I would like to, but I don't know her."

Claude answered, "Take a leap of faith. Is that so difficult? As soon as our team is complete, we will all get to know each other."

"I should have people from all over the world fly here so we can have a cup of coffee?" Bernd asked, indignantly. "I thought you worked with people in virtual teams exclusively over the internet."

"I do. After I get to know them," answered Claude.

Bernd said decisively, "Well, I didn't think we had to do all that. We need every minute to deal with the project data itself and the financing."

"Man, you remind me of the American professor I did the project in Pakistan with. He lost control over everything at one point!"

"So I lost control? Is what you're saying?" Now Bernd was upset.

"Wait, wait, slow down," Claude said. "Nothing has happened, yet. But you should approach this differently. Do it like the American professor did and get a coach or a mentor. The mentor for the Pakistan project was a total expert. The guy's name was Paul. He was an ex-CEO of an international corporation, in his late 40's, and a native Brit, I think. But he has been living in the Caribbean for years and recently in – you won't believe this! – Tibet, in the Himalayas! Seems to be on some sort of spiritual trip, but he's not a nutcase! And he's completely up-to-date technologically. He regularly helps international and multicultural teams work together."

"Thanks, Claude, I think I'll manage," Bernd said, with his voice empty of emotion.

"Yes, of course you'll manage, I don't doubt you one bit. But Paul is a genius! For the project in Pakistan the five of us comprising the team attended a two-day workshop with him. What happened there was unbelievable! We were meeting for the first time, yet after two days we

Paul, a coach with whom Claude has worked before, setup a workshop for Bernd and his team. After the workshop, the team members knew each other well – their likes, dislikes, strengths, and weaknesses –everyone had a clear goal.

knew each other as if we were old friends. Afterwards, everyone had a clear goal of what we were working toward. That was the turning point for us. After that, our performance as a team went through the roof. I suggest you get Paul for a workshop as soon as our team is complete."

Bernd replied: "Claude, I don't need a coach, a mentor, psycho-workshops and especially not some business guru on an esoteric trip! I know my work. Trust me. We have a very tight budget which we must use wisely to get quick results, instead of traveling around the world and wasting time introducing ourselves.

Get to Know Each Other so Trust Can Develop

For Bernd, the first teleconference with a global, virtual team was an unfamiliar challenge. He is highly motivated, wants to risk being plunged in at the deep end and develop personally. But he can't quite step out of his old shoes. He spent the biggest part of his career in hierarchical organizations with predominantly local teams. This shaped him just as much as the "German middle class" with its admittedly pragmatic but often times directive management style.

Bernd wants to trust people like Anne, although he has never met her before. He realizes that this is not easy for him. He is used to being in control. The biggest problem for Bernd in his newly emerging team is his inclination to micromanage. Claude is not quite wrong when he accuses Bernd for his arrogant behavior and know-it-all manner.

If you want to lead a virtual team, you often have to say goodbye to old habits. Trust becomes your greatest asset.

A lot of executives feel like Bernd does. They have one foot in the old world, and one in the new, digitally linked world. The old world provides them with a feeling of security. There, they have knowledge and experience. The new world tempts them, but uncertainty also rises quickly. Can you join such a Skype call from the comfort of your bed? Can anyone speak even if the moderator didn't invite you to? Many managers try to transfer their old knowledge to the new situations. They believe that overall cooperation in virtual, global and multicultural teams works exactly like it did in the local teams they are used to. However, this is a mistake. If you want to lead virtual teams you usually must say goodbye to old habits. This is especially true if virtual teams need to become virtual power teams.

Leaders of Virtual Teams are More "Enablers" than "Managers"

What is the solution for Bernd? How can executives like him change? Initially, it is important to reflect on one's role and attitude. Unlike local teams, virtual teams much first distinguish three questions: the "why," the "what," and the "how." In a nutshell, the "why" is the core task of the executive, the "what" is what the executive works out with their team, and the "how" is up for each team member to decide for themselves.

What does this mean specifically? The "why" is the big goal; the meaning and purpose of it all. Conveying this goal to team members is the leader's responsibility. Bernd has a vision to develop *The "why" is the core task of leadership, the "what" they work together with the team and the "how" each team member decides for himself.* earthquake-proof living conditions for the people in Transmontania. He wants all the members of his virtual team to commit to this goal. At the same time, he does not know the "what" yet. What has to be done in order to reach this goal? What types of houses are ideal? The answer to this question can only be worked out together with his team.

Finally, the "how" requires trust and letting go. Trust that each team member is an expert in his or her field and knows best about the "how," the specific execution of the project. If Anne has experience with crowdfunding and has appropriate contacts at her disposal, then Bernd should let her do her thing. He should ask if she needs anything else from him in order to get started. The leader of the virtual team is more of an "enabler" than a manager. The boss shouldn't interfere when the coast is clear. Bernd is ready to learn this, but the problem is his lack of trust. People activate their largest potential by being trusting each other. Trust, and the focus on an attractive mutual goal, makes a virtual team a virtual power team.

To lead a virtual team, therefore means encouragement, empowerment, and the definition of mutual goals. And how do you build up trust? It starts with getting to know each other.

Personal Relationships in Focus: Why it is Necessary to Connect on a Personal Level

Time and time again, I hear leaders in virtual teams say: "People don't see each other during their worktime anyway. Why go to the effort of arranging personal meetings? If they want to get to know each other, they can make a private appointment."

Getting to know each other is especially important in virtual teams. It doesn't take place organically, however, and needs to be arranged.

This is perhaps the single biggest mistake managers of virtual teams make. They neglect the personal level, because they think *everything* is "virtual." People, however, are not virtual! In virtual teams there is little opportunity for informal communication. During most teleconferences people get straight to the point. In contrast to face-to-face meetings, the participants can't meet at the coffee machine to exchange thoughts before or after the conference. Getting to know each other, talking about personal interests or one's own story – when is this supposed to happen?

Many managers don't address the personal attributes of their virtual team members sufficiently. They don't recognize the individual personal potential of each team member, and often, they are not even aware that this could be a deciding factor in the success of their team. They don't understand that allowing their team to personally connect categorically raises the performance of the entire team! Frequently, members of virtual teams remain anonymous. They are treated as a functional resource to be used when and where they are needed, and they are expected to deliver results at the push of a button. This de-personification causes team members to become demotivated and unengaged. They have no desire to work to their full potential. Precisely because there are no opportunities for personal communication through the geographic distance, it is even more important for virtual team members to get to know each at a personal level.

Attention! In the beginning stage of virtual teams, there are a couple of common mistakes which typically happen. These include exaggerated mistrust, compulsion to control, and micromanagement. The underlying issue is often underestimating how important it is for the team to get to know each other at a personal level. This personal interaction is more important in virtual teams than in teams which meet face-to-face.

Leaders in virtual teams should not expect team members to connect privately on their own. This just does not happen very often. Not helping members get to know each personally will waste valuable time and money. As a matter of fact, the virtual team leader should proactively encourage personal contact within the team and create an environment where the team members can get acquainted as early as possible. They should use the initial excitement and enthusiasm as a momentum for the project to move forward. As a result, as soon as problems arise, team members will already know and trust each other, and they will be able to solve the problems and move forward much more quickly and efficiently. It is therefore wise to make a personal meeting an early and essential priority. This pays off as soon as trust becomes necessary for the project to continue. Occasionally a personal meeting is not an option simply because the team is too big, too widely scattered, or the budget simply doesn't allow for it. In this case, there should be at least one teleconference with a focus on getting personally acquainted.

The Two Sides of Trust

In teams, trust always has two sides: Professional and personal. Professional trust means that you know that a team member has the expertise, knowledge, and experiences necessary to succeed at their tasks. You know that this person can — and will – do the

> *The trust in each team member's personality is equally important as his or her professional competence.*

job given them! Personal trust, on the other hand, is trust in the person him- or herself. Personal trust can only take place after you have had the chance to get to know a team member personally. Only then do you know their strengths and weaknesses. Only then can you evaluate their behavior. You can challenge and motivate them. You know what gives them joy and energy, and you know what discourages them. You can communicate with them much more effectively if something goes wrong, and you are less likely to jump to conclusions if they for some reason have a bad day.

To summarize: The better you know your team members at a personal level, the better you can support and lead them from a distance.

Questions to Reflect Upon:

- Do you know the personal interests of your virtual team members? Do you know some of the things that they have experienced in life? Do you know their strengths and weaknesses?

- How can you create an environment in which team members can personally express themselves and use their talents to help the virtual team to be more creative and innovative?

- How can you keep up personal contact to the members of your virtual team, and how will this help you and your team succeed?

A Workshop Delivers the Breakthrough

My first international project as a manager aimed to establish Shared Services for 20 European countries. The goal was to transfer the IT Management to global shared services. After the initial enthusiasm, the project became more and more tenuous. I realized that this was due in part to my style. I exerted too much pressure on the team, and the team didn't follow me.

I decided to arrange an all-day workshop with all the coworkers, and I had everyone introduce themselves. The personal introduction had not worked in written form or via telecommunication. After the workshop, the team's performance curve went up drastically. Confidence increased and team members communicated with each other much more effectively. We got results, and I made sure that we continued having those personal meetings!

As a result, I learned early in my career that personal interaction makes an enormous difference. Today, I advise companies not to wait for a crisis. They should have a workshop for personal interaction as soon as the virtual team is created. If for organizational or budgetary reasons, it is not possible to carry out such a workshop face-to-face, they should at least hold a virtual meeting with the focus on getting to know each other personally. With appropriate software, the participants can even show drawings, photos, and videos. And if your team is too big for a joint workshop? Then limit yourself initially to the core leadership team and empower them to grow strong personal relationships with each other.

How to Create a Great Workshop

For effective and inspiring workshops for your team to get to know each other, I recommend a tried and proven method which I have been using in my work for a long time. Let each team member introduce themselves with two prepared slides. On the first slide they should draw their professional "Lifeline" and on the other slide, their personal "Lifeline."

As an alternative to prepared slides with PowerPoint, Keynote or Prezi, the team members can draw their lifelines in person on flipchart pages or through projections on an interactive whiteboard. The focus of this exercise are "lifelines" themselves as a way of getting to know the person. Anyone who would like to may overlap and compare both lines at the end. This can be especially exciting! Let the most courageous participants begin, and soon, everyone will want to show their lifelines.

The personal "Lifeline" is key for getting to know each other. It is exciting to compare professional and personal lifelines.

For the most part, the professional lifeline is not as interesting as the personal one. Nevertheless, I am always surprised by what comes out. One participant wanted to become an actor, for example, and another was formerly a journalist. Many others would never have chosen the path they ended up taking. A lot of interesting topics for conversation were now on the table.

Method: Create a workshop and ask each team member to present themselves with a professional and personal lifeline, focusing on their greatest successes and greatest challenges.

The personal lifeline is most important. I usually encourage participants to present both their proudest moments and their biggest challenges here. One of the proudest moments is perhaps a medal in sports or a prize as a hobby cook. In one team, I once had the winner of the World Championship for remote-controlled model boats – never even knowing that there was such a thing! For the greatest challenge, another team member listed the education of an autistic child. This was very touching for everyone. By the way, sharing photos and videos is often particularly helpful. Thanks to smartphones, this part of the workshop can be very spontaneous.

In one of my workshops, there was a young man who was a member of a German non-profit organization. His professional "lifeline" continued steadily upward, while the personal had some very low points (see figure). His parents parted when he was five years old. This is the first downward spiral in the drawing. He talked about how he was first a class spokesman, then active in local politics, and finally had his "breakthrough" in a discussion with Bundestag delegates. When he wanted to tell his mother about it that evening, however, he found her dissolved in tears. She had been diagnosed with cancer that very day. The personal line of his life continued steeply downward.

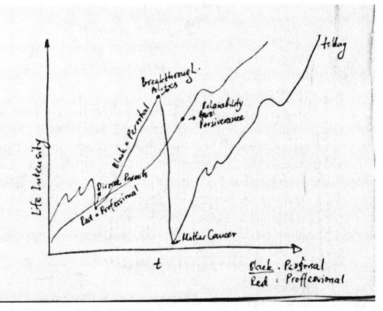

Illustration 2: Workshop example of a professional and personal life line

The team members recognize what they have already done in the past. This gives them courage for all future challenges.

The young man could have chosen to pursue his political career but stayed close to his mother instead. If they did not see each other every day, he called or connected via Skype. Although his personal line of life was almost zero again, it was this situation in which he developed the strength of character and resilience that his team members later appreciated so much about him. Through the workshop, everyone on his team knew about this.

This is one example of why this workshop is so important.

What is it about this workshop that helps people get to know each other so easily? The team members present themselves with their ups and downs. They focus especially on their greatest successes, that is, on moments that make them particularly proud. That takes a lot of courage! It suddenly becomes visible to everyone what has been achieved by individuals on the team and what challenges are already mastered. People feel a sense of pride and realize that they've done so much in the past, that they will now be able to cope with the challenges that will arise in this new situation.

Within 10-15 minutes each team member also discovers what touches their heart. And every team member learns important things about every colleague. The seed for fertile interpersonal relationships has been planted. Even local teams, who had already worked together for 15 years, were amazed at what they could learn about each other.

Possible agenda at a start-up workshop:

1. Lifeline exercise

2. Discover personal strengths

3. Develop and define goals

4. Summarize goals as a roadmap

5. Set rules for structured communication

6. Personal commitment of each team member

Getting to personally know each other is not the only factor in your team's success, but it creates the basis for trust in a virtual team. The task of the management is to further promote the personal contact of the team members across the geographical distance. The workshop makes it possible to recognize the unique strengths of each team member through their respective professional and personal lifelines. On this basis, each individual is committed to personal goals that match thier strengths. Each person is unique and they make their own indispensable contribution to the success of a virtual power team. Everyone is a star and can light up with confidence when strengths and goals match.

Interview with Thorsten Broese

Thorsten Broese was a top manager and most recently Group Head of IT Services with an international corporation of around 60,000 employees and an annual turnover of almost 20 billion Euros. His company is represented in 180 countries around the world and headquar-

tered in the UK. Thorsten's desk is in Kuala Lumpur. From there, he reports directly to the CIO (Chief Information Officer) in the Group's Management Board. More than 42,000 employees across the globe work with IT every day, for which Thorsten was responsible. His greatest successes include the unification of global IT and the introduction of cloud services. Thorsten has led global teams with stakeholders in more than 150 countries. Through these projects, companies have saved hundreds of millions of euros. What impresses me most about Thorsten is the modesty he has preserved. With this attitude, he treats every single team member in the world with great respect.

Who are you and what are you doing? Just describe yourself!

I am 52 years old, married, have two sons and live in a city near Hamburg. In addition to my professional and family life, I like to be in nature and keep myself physically fit with running, cycling and hiking. As a German, I love fast cars, good food (more than sauerkraut and sausages), and good red wine!

We need to think and work more in networks. This automatically leads us to teams without borders and flat hierarchies

Many, many years ago, I studied mathematics and computer science. Since then I have worked with different companies. This ranges from very small companies with fewer than five employees to companies with more than 60,000 employees. I also was self-employed for a while.

In IT, I initially had different roles - from the analyst to the database administrator, to the programmer and the project manager. But over the past 20 years, I have been mostly involved in managing global teams.

A few months ago, I decided to change my way of working and took a Sabbatical. There is still a lot that I want to do, and I do not want to wait until I am old and retired to achieve these goals. I believe that the traditional way of working and the careers of big corporations are no longer the best answers to the challenges of our world. In the future we need to think and work more in networks. This automatically leads us to teams without borders and flat hierarchies: to virtual teams.

What are your experiences with virtual teams?

I had been part of virtual teams at the end of the 1990s, with companies in the USA, the UK, the Netherlands, Italy, and Germany. We worked together for customers all over the world. At that time, it was mainly project work. We developed and supported IT systems. During the late 1990s, Open Source became quite popular in IT, and for the first time, virtual teams were able to show and share what they were doing.

Since those early days, I have gained more and more experience with virtual teams, going increasingly beyond pure project teams. I also had virtual teams within the line organization. It always crossed geographical boundaries, time zones, and cultures. It ended with my last team distributing to over 60 different countries and even more cities across the globe.

For me, virtual teams are much more important than the fact that the employees are spread across different countries and the team members come from different backgrounds. To mention another aspect: the teams are now not only in different places but also are rarely part of the same organization. In many projects, you have permanent employees from your own organization as well as freelancers, consultants, employees of service providers and partners, and very often, customers.

"New leadership" for me means that I know how I influence freelancers, consultants, employees of service providers and customers.

I've spent over ten years in IT services where outsourcing plays a huge role. There, a management must be able to rely heavily on external companies. Often one must deal with two or three times as many employees in the partner company as in one's own company. "New leadership" means that I know as a leader how I can influence these people and lead them. Everyone is equally important in achieving our goals.

Which of your successes as a leader and entrepreneur make you particularly proud?

Over the past five years, our corporation has been undergoing major changes in IT. Initially, we had very different ways to support our more than 40,000 users in 180 countries around the world. Our goal at that time was to centralize almost all data centers, networks, call centers, software services and so on, as much as possible. We outsourced services to external partners, adapted processes, and made the entire organization more efficient. This not only saved a lot of money but also allowed for a slimmer and more agile organization. This was about future-proofing technologies and services, and this enormous change had to be done in real time, without the business processes being interrupted. A kind of open heart operation that only a very small number of companies in the world have managed thus far.

The program involved a few hundred people in many different locations, with very different backgrounds, and across many corporate boundaries. This was a pure virtual power teams culture! Just twelve months ago, we successfully completed this program and achieved the expected results without the business being disturbed in any way. On the contrary, the service quality and what we call the silent operation of the IT had significantly improved. It was a great success story and one that was only possible with a great virtual team. The team was connected through overriding goals, outstanding commitment at all levels, and a whole host of silent heroes on the ground, not to mention the big parties with which we celebrated our successes.

How do you motivate your team?

I think before you can motivate a team or an individual, you need to make sure the basics are right. For example, you should create an environment where people dare to express themselves freely, try new things, and move boundaries. I strongly believe in such a positive motivating environment. Employees who are afraid will not deliver their maximum performance and are difficult to motivate.

People like to be involved, so I try to share as much knowledge and information as possible with employees. This creates an environment of trust in which all team members can share information and knowledge.

In many teams, frustration spreads because the goals are not clear. To avoid confusion, targets must be crystal clear and consistent with the company's higher objectives. If possible, the strategic and annual team goals as well as the individual goals should be developed together with the team.

If it is possible, the strategic and annual team goals as well as the individual goals should be developed together with the team.

It should also be ensured that great work is recognized and rewarded for each individual. I do not mean money at this point. I simply mean giving as much praise as possible, preferably in front of many other people. At the same time, poor performance and problems should be addressed openly but in private, either one-on-one or in a small group by only those who are affected of the problem. Too often I have seen the opposite: people get praised privately and criticized publicly.

It is clear to me that teams and individual people like competition and challenge as long as there is a positive environment and enough support so that everyone has a chance to win. This really prompts people to go the extra mile.

Last, but not least, when you set challenging goals, you should motivate the team to break boundaries, and when it comes to completion, make sure you celebrate the success. Allow everyone to have lots of fun. This creates the best prerequisite for motivating team experience, which binds team members even more closely together.

How do you make sure no one is hiding within the team?

This is a very good question, and even more important when working in a virtual team that is scattered in many places. Notably, people are different in their personality and culture; while some are extroverted, others are quieter. However, the diversity of the team is one of the greatest resources. Be careful not to pre-judge someone just because they do not dominate in meetings or telephone conferences. They may be some of your strongest team members.

One should clarify what the team goals are and what each individual is expected to contribute. It should be ensured that each person, the team, and the team leader regularly assess the team's progress, demonstrate the need for improvement, and ensure that team members support each other until they are successful.

It is also normal that you have to manage other activities at the same time and solve other problems. This provides a good opportunity to ask individual people on the team to take on additional responsibilities. People who may be quiet or prone to hide should be approached before meetings and asked to take on these additional tasks.

People who may be quiet or tend to hide, should be approached before meetings and offered additional tasks.

If, however, the person asked refuses to help out in team meetings or to take on additional tasks, it is the responsibility of the executive to take action with this person. If nothing works to encourage this team member to take on more responsibility or become more engaged, it is best for everyone involved to find a new role for that person.

There are a few things that are important when working in virtual teams. Since you cannot go to each team member's neighboring office, team members who work in the same building or at least in the same city have a higher responsibility. Real A+ Teams and Virtual Power teams only work when everyone delivers the maximum performance.

Inferior performance is no longer just a problem for executives. It must be openly addressed by the whole team.

Last, but not least, not everyone may be able to sit alone at home, be part of a team which is on the other side of the earth, and deliver great results. Although team leaders using the methods they find in your book will experience a lot of success and will be able to guide and motivate their teams, each individual needs a high degree of discipline and self-motivation for the team to succeed. This is particularly true when people work at home all by themselves.

What was the secret of your company's success?

This question is difficult to answer, and I do not think there is such a thing as a secret. I do think, however, that I had success in my work environment because I believe in people. In the world of IT, there are a lot of tools, processes, and rules. We are the masters of hardware and software, and we have maxed all other departments in our companies. Yet in the end, everything revolves around people and how to lead people.

There is a certain risk in our virtual world that we only focus on products and processes, and that the human aspect comes up too short. This is because it is often difficult to lead people across a geographical distance. For his reason, I have always tried to be authentic and open. This has usually created a trusting environment where people feel safe to express themselves and share their experiences and ambitions with others. This is an environment in which no one is discriminated against because of sex, age or skin color.

In this way, I have always succeeded in bringing together colorful teams in which there was a strong cohesion and which was based on trust. In addition, I am a very result-oriented person. So it's not just that we're all happy, but it's first and foremost about creating the conditions to set ambitious goals to reach the next level with our team.

How do you ensure effective communication when your employees are scattered? What means of communication do you use?

I work with a combination of few face-to-face meetings and regular virtual meetings. If there are very challenging goals for the team, or a difficult process of change which involves a lot of change for the organization as a whole, strong links between team members, team spirit, and trust are essential.

While in the day-to-day business we are able to do a lot of things by virtual means, I am firmly convinced that some face-to-face meetings are necessary to ensure team cohesion, especially at the beginning of a difficult journey, or when a new team comes together.

The form of the face-to-face meeting does not exist as a set recipe. It is rather a combination of interactive group meetings, workshops, individual talks, team developments

I firmly believe that some real meetings are needed to ensure team cohesion, especially at the beginning of a difficult journey.

and not least, of parties and events to celebrate a great success. Although personal meetings offer the best opportunity to bring everyone involved to the same level and share information, I have increasingly focused on the informal part of these meetings and visits. A great team can be created only if you know the respective personalities and the experiences of the other team members. Personal meetings, therefore, are a great opportunity to learn about the careers of the people, their culture, their personalities, their dreams, their ambitions, and their fears. This happens, however, only if the leader himself also opens up and reveals something personal.

While many people love to visit a company headquarters, it is equally important as leader to find the employees where they live and work. Out in the field, people are usually more open-minded, and if you keep your eyes and ears open, you will get a lot of insights that you would never get in the headquarters.

If there are only a few personal meetings, it is even more important to communicate regularly with all employees around the world. We always had a communication plan for the whole year, which we could adjust if necessary. An example of this might be when events occurred that required immediate communication. The plan should be a directive but not an inflexible requirement.

We have used a combination of video conferencing (podcast, web), newsletters, and personal messages to communicate across the enterprise. Nothing really new or special! Nevertheless, here is what I found that worked well:

For large telephone, video or web conferencing, one should remember to pay attention to the time zones, the time shifts, and the deadlines of the parties involved. In the case of the people in Asia and Australia as well as in North and South America, we sometimes offered two different dates on the same day. We recorded the conference and those who could not attend virtually, could watch the conference later on a centralized website.

Conferences, in which several hundred employees are dialing, cannot be carried out in a dialogue or as a question-and-answer format, but there are ways to make it interactive. For example, people can ask questions by e-mail, messenger, or other communication channels. These questions in turn, can be addressed during the conference. An alternative is to organize the telephone conference so that it is part of a face-to-face meeting in a larger branch office. This way, there are people in that space and people online who are discussing the given topics.

Employees that work in a virtual environment don't have the opportunity of getting to know each other as people. Humans, however, have emotions and need more than facts and information. This means that as a leader, you should always think about how to create an environment in which authentic and personal communication can occur. For example, every two months I sent my employees a personal message in which I reported about current business developments, described initiatives, and addressed successes and failures. Each time I also wrote a paragraph about myself, whether it concerned my family, sports or vacation. Every leader can think about what's important to them and what they would like to share.

Humans have emotions and need more than facts and information. You must always think about how to make communication more humane.

There was also always personal, individual communication with us. We constantly encouraged our employees to give us feedback and suggestions for improvement. We created an environment in which middle management wasn't sacred, and where employees could get past it and turn to higher management. It is important to listen exclusively to the employees and not to make any decisions that are the responsibility of the middle management. If there is an environment like that, all communication channels should be open: phone, e-mail, messengers, web and video conferences. Different people happen to prefer different communication channels for a variety of reasons. It is important that you are approachable and available as team leader and that this not only applies to you but also your entire leading team. Otherwise, one of the bosses is going to drown in calls and mails.

How did you control your employees? How did you get everyone to do their best?

I think much of this has already been addressed. I will list a few more aspects that are important for people in leadership positions.

Executives are often afraid that employees they can't see don't do their work. That's why they sometimes end up as micromanagers and control freaks.

Many of our current day management methods originated in the first half of the last century. Back then it was all about an army of workers that had to do manual labor in strict time to keep a factory up and running. During this time, work was unhealthy, boring and frustrating. That's why there were controlling mechanisms to "motivate" employees. These made sense at that time. Today, however, we don't want people's arms and legs, we want their heads. That's why there is no need to control whether someone is physically present at their desk. Because even then, they might not be present in their thoughts.

Making time and attendance a basis of management doesn't create a real value. You should go the extra mile and define clear goals. It's about numbers and results. Then you can see how employees reach their goals and this, the achieving of goals, is what the leader should control.

There is no need to control whether someone is physically present. A leader must control goal attainment.

Therefore, it is important to regularly check with the team about where things stand. It should be enough to do this once a month, unless an extraordinary situation occurs. (For example, if an employee needs help or you are in a difficult phase yourself.) I also advise to look at your goals regularly with the entire team because then you can see who is on time, and who isn't within reach of the goals. You can then redistribute the tasks if necessary.

The team leader should be aware that they are responsible for the team and the team members. They should choose the right people for the right objectives. While there is a lot of freedom and flexibility in a virtual team, there are still duties and responsibilities for each member. If team members have a problem with this freedom and flexibility and if they need daily motivation and control, then I advise you to replace these people as soon as possible. Their lack of motivation and self-discipline will affect the entire team negatively. Having the right people in a virtual team is even more important than in a local team, and if you want an A-team then you need to define high standards and enforce them.

All in all, controlling and micromanagement isn't the job of the leader, neither in a virtual team nor in any other team. Their job is about choosing the right people, setting clear goals and motivating the team. When this happens, the leader spends most of their time working as an enabler for the team. This means making sure that there are no obstacles in the team's way.

How can you ensure that employees go the extra mile and that the team is more than a sum of its parts?

Quite simply, people like learning and growing. People like challenges, and they would like to challenge and surpass themselves. People like competition, and they like to win. People will always work together whenever it is about going the extra mile and achieving incredible goals, if they get the credit for it and their work is appreciated.

If I can draw a larger picture, let me say this: goals and ambitions are the key. The team leader should make sure that there are challenges, that people explore unfamiliar terrain and leave their comfort zones. If, however, the goals are unrealistic and can't be reached, resistance, frustration, and sarcasm will spread, and there will be very bad results.

The executive must make sure that there are challenges, that people explore unfamiliar terrain and leave their comfort zones.

I like to use the high jump as an example. If somebody usually manages 2.00 meters and their record is 2.03 meters, then 2.03 meters isn't a challenging goal. If I demand 2.30 meters instead, then that person will think I'm crazy and won't even try. If I present 2.06 meters, they will train harder and be motivated. And if I set 2.10 meters as the goal while hiring a coach that will tell them how to reach this goal, motivation will be extremely high. So, I set a high goal and then go to all the lengths to ensure that my employees can reach it.

It also works for me to maintain a little healthy competition between the teams. This includes boosting sales more efficiently, achieving a higher customer satisfaction rate, or meeting the service level standards. You should, however, keep an eye out as to whether everything is fair, and you should make sure that the team members support each other if necessary.

In addition, there should always be something to win. To go the extra mile and achieve extraordinary goals, there needs to be a reward. There are different ways you can go about doing this, and money can definitely be a factor. Better yet, team events in one special location, an unforgettable party or a prize that is awarded in a festive way are great motivators. In short: It's about success and celebration.

How do you evaluate the meaning of virtual and boundless teams in the future?

Since the 1990's, the playing field worldwide is level. Political boundaries and other limitations have dissolved. Information is spreading like wildfire. Businesses and consumers think globally and the best

norm in the future, and this will lead to better and faster results. people from all over the planet can work for the best companies.

In addition, the good old days when people worked for a company for 20 years or longer, is over. Many businesses today don't even exist for 20 years. Everything is much more project-oriented, and for *Virtual teams, flat hierarchies and natural leadership will be the* that you need employees, partners, networks and teams for 6-24 months. After that, a new team emerges.

Businesses are focusing on their core competencies more and more. Everything else is taken care of by external partners, advisors and networks.

For me, all of this is only the beginning of a longer system. Virtual teams, flat hierarchies and natural leadership will be the norm in the future. And this will lead to better and faster results than even the most dedicated in-house team can deliver today.

Chapter 2

Bringing Together a Great Team
Leads to a Phenomenal Success

Story

Bernd woke up from a dream just before half past six; a warm feeling of happiness flowed through him. In his dream he saw the happy, smiling faces of the residents of Transmontania. A little boy was smiling cheek to cheek and pointing to a house much more solid and robust than their previous one. He was looking up at the man nearby and asking, "Papa, is this our new house?" Bernd felt himself break into a smile as he visualized the pictures once more.

Suddenly, his mind felt as if someone had pressed a button, and immediately an urgent "to-do" list seized his thoughts. The first item was "Research Crowdfunding: Platforms and Best Practices."

Bernd felt tension spread throughout his body; the pleasant feeling from the dream was pushed aside by a vibrating nervousness. "Come on Bernd," the entrepreneur said softly to himself, "You've mastered more complex challenges." But trying to talk himself into relaxing only made him more stressed.

Bernd took his iPad from his nightstand, opened it, and googled "Crowdfunding." Skimming through the search results, Bernd recalled Anne's remark about knowing a crowdfunding expert in her network, someone she had worked with on several occasions. "Nevertheless," he said to himself, "I need to understand what this is all about," and he kept on reading.

Scarcely five minutes had passed when the other "to do's" on his list began vying for his attention:

- Research MOOC

- Plan the next Skype conference with the team

- Accelerate progress and find solutions at the construction site in Frankfurt

As Bernd stirred in bed, the light of his iPad woke his wife, Wiebke. She gently turned and kissed his cheek.

Bernd notes that it is not possible to lead the team, to make his own contributions to the project, and to learn about this new area of expertise at the same time. He feels overwhelmed.

Bernd's thoughts were spinning. "I've got to go. I've got to spend all day today doing research, but I just don't have the time. I hate it when others on my team already know more than I do."

"Why?" Wiebke responded. "Just be happy."

But Bernd was feeling overwhelmed, and it was only 5:30 a.m.! He quickly showered, dressed, and made himself a cup of coffee. He grabbed the milk out of the refrigerator and poured it into his cup. Looking at the clock, he quickly chugged down the lukewarm coffee and went to his garage. It was still dark when he climbed into his BMW.

Fortunately, it was too early for rush hour, so there weren't too many cars on the road. He quickly changed lanes to race to his office, as if changing lanes would take hours off of his commute. Once he arrived at the office, he parked his car and walked out of the garage. For the first time in a long time, he felt absolutely overwhelmed, and the day had just begun.

It was gray but dry in the port city of Hamburg. Bernd sat in the dim light of his desk lamp in front of his computer. Suddenly, with its now familiar sound, the Skype logo appeared on Bernd's screen, and the Claude's cheerful face popped up. "How can Claude always be in such a good mood," thought Bernd as he clicked the green button to accept the call.

"Hey Bernd," Claude said immediately, without pausing for small talk. "Remember the MOOC professor from New York I mentioned in our last conversation? Well, I spoke with him this evening, and he wants to support us! He's ready to join our next team call to define the parameters, and then he's ready to be on board!"

"I'm not that far along, Claude," Bernd said hesitantly. "Researching MOOC has been on my list for a week, but I still haven't gotten there. Without the research, I cannot define any parameters."

"Relax. Let the professor make suggestions. We know what kind of houses we want. How he designs them using his MOOC format is entirely up to him."

"Is this how you handled your Pakistan project?"

"Yes, he knows his stuff."

"Well, our next telephone conference is next Wednesday," Bernd added, "I am just planning it now. Please see that you get all of the information about the MOOC from the professor by then, and you can briefly present it at the next conference." *The team has been ready to start, but Bernd is not ready to let go. He wants the others to wait until he, as the boss, has already researched and planned everything.*

"All right, I'll do my best! Do you see what we are doing? It's like putting together pieces of a puzzle. Next week, Anne will be able to introduce her crowdfunding guru at the conference. Then our team will be mobilized and can start delivering. My hands are itching to get this underway!"

Bernd: "But I'm not yet finished with the research, let alone the planning. Let me decide next Wednesday during the conference whether we really can do crowdfunding, or whether we should go through the banks or through private equity."

"No problem, you're the boss! Just know that Anne and I are keen to start! We both are bringing very experienced people into the team, real stars. As long as we set clear goals we do not have to plan everything in great detail. Try and take it easy. Once we find the best in the field and they commit to our goal, you can let them take off and fly."

"Ok, ok" said Bernd, still feeling overwhelmed. "I am sure you are right."

The rest of Bernd's day was frantic. At noon he flew to Frankfurt for a few hours. Just seeing the construction site gave him a much needed boost. He met with his customer and team leaders, made some decisions on the spot, and was feeling much better by the end of the day.

On the way home he checked his e-mail and saw a note from Anne:

> *Crowdfunding expert ready to join! Linda, my colleague*
> *from Cambridge, has been running crowdfunding cam-*
> *paigns for the past 5 years. She is fascinated by our project*
> *and very eager to join us. I have worked with her several*
> *times and she's brilliant. She is not only very experienced*
> *and committed, but also very well connected in the inter-*
> *national financial world. By the way, she is currently living*
> *in her homeland in southern Nigeria. There, she is work-*
> *ing on several non-profit projects to improve infrastructure.*
> *Should I invite Linda to our next telephone conference?*

Bernd continued to stare at the text. From the loud speaker he heard the announcement, *"Ladies and gentlemen, your Lufthansa flight to Hamburg is now ready for boarding,"* but Bernd couldn't move. The meeting in Frankfurt had gone according to his plans. Everyone on the site accepted his suggestions and ideas. He was glad his virtual team was taking initiative, but he was also reminded of how far behind he was. He hadn't even begun to research crowdfunding resources.

I'm the bottleneck here, thought Bernd resignated. He stood up slowly and got in line at the gate. "Okay," thought Bernd, feeling his muscles tighten, "I'll just work an hour later tonight." As he thought this, he felt dread come over his body at the thought of turning his computer back on.

At midday on Wednesday, the air was heavy with an impending storm. With only an hour before the telephone conference, Bernd decided to skip lunch to review the agenda:

- Government request – scope, budget, timing

- Financing – crowdfunding and World Bank – Linda

- Design – Claude/ input from the MOOC Professor, definition of the parameters

- Building Teams – feedback from Anne

Promptly at 1 p.m. Bernd set up a Skype conference with Anne and Claude. "There's got to be a more professional way to set up a conference call than this," thought Bernd as he clicked on the green button.

First Claude appeared with a "Good morning from Canada! This time I have showered, shaved, and I even put on a fresh shirt just for you all!"

Then, with her pleasant voice and her Oxford accent, Anne answered, "Good morning, Bernd. Good afternoon, Claude." Anne was wearing a colorful dress, her hair was neatly arranged in a top knot.

Bernd replied, "Hello, Anne. Hello, Claude. Glad to see you after so much e-mailing. Will Linda be able to join us today?"

"Yes, Bernd," replied Anne. "She's ready to join any moment now".

"Claude, do you have the information from the MOOC professor?"

"Yes, Boss!"

"Then, let's get started" said Bernd. He asked if everyone had received a copy of the agenda, and then he asked Anne to report on the state of things.

First, Anne confirmed that the site for the houses has been approved. There were volunteers and members of the army clearing out the rubble from the earthquake. There is, however, a problem. The World Bank is not willing to give us as much funding as we had hoped, a fact which has now been confirmed by the finance minister of Transmontania. Additional funding will definitely be needed.

We are looking for experienced, local builders, and for the additional financing Crowdfunding seems very suitable. If it's okay with you two, I would like to connect Linda now, so she can tell us more about her crowdfunding ideas."

Bernd and Claude agreed in unison.

"Hi Anne! Good day, gentlemen! My name is Linda Ogedeng-be-Smith. I have been responsible for financing various infrastructure projects in Africa. Recently, we've done this predominantly through crowdfunding. I think crowdfunding would also be very feasible in this case. Despite the global recession, people are still willing to give money for a good cause, and the West will also benefit from the rising purchasing power in Asia.

One challenge I see, however, is that we will have to do a public relations campaign for the initiative, and we cannot rely on Crowdfunding platforms alone."

Bernd interrupted, "Linda, how can you guarantee that the money will come together? If it doesn't, we'll be standing there with empty hands."

Linda replied most confidently: "So far, I have always reached my financing targets. In some cases, we've needed to get additional assistance from my worldwide financial network, and in some cases we've had to use intelligent positioning and promotional campaigns to get the job done. Most of the time, we've succeeded through a combination of both of these things."

"Excuse me, Linda," Bernd said with a full voice. "You will surely understand how important this point is for us. Can you provide me with a detailed financing plan where I can see what steps are necessary to reach the goals you want to achieve?"

Linda responded with calm confidence: "Bernd, the key steps are clear, and I am happy to describe them. A detailed plan, however, is not practical at this stage. Our approach may

Bernd asks Linda, the crowd-funding expert, to give him a detailed financing plan. Other-wise he cannot trust her.

change depending on the feedback from my network or the first reactions of potential investors. If you are willing to trust me, I'll adapt our strategy and tactics along the way, and show how we will reach our goal."

Bernd felt nervous again. He did not understand the mechanisms of crowdfunding because he had not had the time to research it. Now he was dependent on a foreign person whom he did not know at all and her ominous network. In addition, reaction of the possible donors was also still completely open. Bernd did not like that at all.

Bernd replied, "Well, Linda, please describe your plan in as much detail as possible, and let's have a one-on-one call so I can decide."

Linda asked, "Will Monday of next week be alright?"

Bernd responded, feeling somewhat relieved, "Yes, let's call at 2 in the afternoon, please."

Bernd felt more sure of himself now. "Okay, ladies and gentlemen," he said, "The next point on the agenda are the blueprints for earth-quake-resistant residential buildings. As we all remember, we are plan-ning to hire thousands of students worldwide in a mass-online course."

When he expressed this fact, Bernd felt a sense of inner unrest. "Claude knows a professor who has organized these MOOCs and has had great success in Pakistan. Claude, can you briefly explain how a MOOC functions and how it will help us develop blueprints for our construction plan?"

"But surely!" came Claude's happy response over the digital platform. "The MOOC we will utilize will be titled "Designing Earthquake-Resis-tant, Cost-Effective Residential Structures for Transmontania." This will be led by a friend of mine who is a professor at the City University in New York, someone who cooperates intensively with the UN, and also leads other MOOCs in tandem.

Our MOOC will last six weeks. Students will be given video training on modern design principles and practice, and complete a number of assignments along the way. There is a team of University professors to review the students' work and give feedback online. The students will work in groups of 5 -10 self-organizing teams, and they will gradually develop a complete design of houses with a focus on resistance to natural catastrophes while also improving cost efficiency. The best designs are then chosen by the professors, and by a vote of all students. These designs will be made available to us free of charge. Do you have questions?"

"When I consider that you've done this successfully for your Pakistani projects I am happy to go for it," Anne replied. "One question that comes to mind is how to involve local builders, and how do we ensure that our tradi-

The MOOC will deliver thousands of architectural designs within six weeks. Will they meet the necessary requirements and take into consideration local traditions?

tions and customary materials are taken into account - before it is too late?"

"Great question, Anne," Claude responded. "I'll ask the professor to include local representatives from Transmontania in the MOOC as consultants and participants from the start, so they have first-hand experience with the process and visibility on the assignments submitted, and can provide feedback. I will get back to you on this by the end of the week."

Bernd thought to himself "Oh no, yet another interface to manage: architectural students and traditional builders from Transmontania!"

Then Bernd asked Anne to address the last item on the agenda: Status of the construction teams. Apparently, the government was finalizing another tender for the local builders; since it was an emergency situation, these negotiations were in urgent proceedings. The main contractor where Bernd's team was bidding would have some visibility and input to the selection process. Anne was confident that soon there would be enough builders ready to proceed. Many foreign workers from China, however, would be needed since Transmontania would be overburdened with the scope of this project.

Bernd summarized the actions of the meeting, thanked everyone, and set the next group call for three weeks out.

It was two in the afternoon in Hamburg. The call had lasted only one hour, but it felt like a lifetime with so many things unfolding simultaneously. Bernd felt his hunger pangs rising again, but he was too tense to eat. He wanted to speak with Claude one more time.

He pressed the green Skype button, and Claude picked up.

"Bernd, you telephone terrorist! Would you please let me have time for breakfast? I am so hungry and excited now. We have such a brilliant bunch of people. I feel that we are going to have a great time together and build excellent homes that will be the envy of the world!"

Bernd replied, "I just need five minutes – then you can have your breakfast and I will have my lunch.

I want to share your enthusiasm, but in truth I feel exactly the opposite. First, we are going ahead with crowdfunding when I have no clue how Linda can deliver the required funding, nor do I understand how it works.

Second, we go with the MOOC, which I do not understand, either. I can't see a guarantee for the results, and now we have to include local builders in the process!

I don't see how to manage this, not understanding these processes sufficiently and not having a detailed plan. How do I keep track of who is responsible for what, much less be certain that we are providing what is needed?"

Bernd remains distrustful because he does not personally know everyone involved in the project nor has he any detailed plans. Uncertainties are difficult to bear.

Claude replied, "Relax Bernd, you are over thinking. You are so lucky to have a team of stars. Everyone has done their bit in a global environment and understands the usual uncertainties and ambiguities. Don't worry so much about the details of *how*. They will figure it out. They and their respective networks. You have brought them together to help a great cause, and they are all eager to achieve this goal. Now, with the help of everyone on the team, we are shaping *what* has to be done. It is essential to let them decide on the *how*. Do not waste your time over-managing. Trust, have confidence in them, and you will be amazed."

Bernd responded, "I wish I had your trust."

Claude then asked: "Bernd, why don't we plan for all of us to get together in person for a couple of days. Once you know them personally, you will be much more inclined to trust them - to see the people behind the tasks that they are fulfilling. And we can use the opportunity to nail down the individual goals at the same time."

Bernd quickly stated: "We are not going anywhere before we sort out the financing and the crowdfunding."

Claude: "Right! I am glad you are getting more open to the process. Let's go and get some food!"

This is How Virtual Power Teams are Created Today

In the past, it was not enough to have brilliant ideas and great visions. Those who did not know the right people had little chance of making their dream a reality.

Today, it is no longer a problem to attract experts from all over the world. Everyone is connected through the Internet and can be reached at any time. People present their skills on their own websites and in social networks such as LinkedIn or XING. Through e-mail and messaging services, everyone is always available for everyone else. It is typical for each expert to have a network of other experts, with whom they are also connected through the Internet. Anyone who does not move forward can immediately get in touch with someone else. It has never been so easy to put together a team of global experts.

This means that today it is important to have innovative ideas and visions. The more fascinating the vision and the more rewarding the goal, the greater the likelihood that the best of the best around the world will want to get involved and join your team. More and more, the rule is that a good idea automatically attracts the best people.

The challenge for today's entrepreneurs, managers and non-profit organizations is not so much to find the best; the challenge is to unite them to establish an environment of collaboration, an environment where trust rules, and where everyone will go the extra mile in order to achieve the team's objective. One must create a truly collaborative structure.

Bernd is someone who recognizes opportunity and has the desire to follow through with it. In our story, the most important point of contact for Bernd is Claude. Claude is a typical networker or

The challenge today is no longer to find the best people; instead, it is to inspire the best people for an idea or mission.

"connector" (a person with rich network). He is someone who has many active contacts with whom he likes to maintain interpersonal relationships, even if they do not always benefit him directly. One of Claude's favorite sentences is: "Maybe we can do something together sometime." This "sometime" may be in the near future or many years later. It is also possible that this "sometime" never comes, but Claude keeps his contacts just in case. The networker makes contacts, so to speak, on stock.

It is also very important to understand that when you are compiling a virtual team, you should not only look at who has the best references or the most experience, but also who is the most inspired.

In this team, Linda, from Africa, is one such inspired and inspiring member. She is a top expert, and she was immediately enthusiastic about the project. Her enthusiasm is contagious, and she initiates a strong spirit which others connect to. When everyone feels that enthusiasm the team as a whole becomes more than the sum of its individual parts. When team members all over the world are drawn into the gravitational force of a vision of the goals they want to achieve together, an upward spiral arises, carrying them forward. This group, although they are spread around the world, then has a collective power that unites them towards their mutual cause and team goal, and they can establish and maintain a winning spirit. They are able to tackle all challenges to reach their goal.

Relate to Each Other on a Personal Level

You already know one success factor for power teams from Chapter 1: Relating to each other at a personal level!

In developing your virtual power team, it is vitally important to get to know each team member personally, so that you are aware of the differences among individuals on the team. People have individual styles of thinking, processing information, and are motivated for different reasons to participate in a project. There are sophisticated personality profiles that help you analyze the character of your team members. Sometimes, however, the exercise of personal and professional "Lifelines" that we discussed in Chapter one is more than enough to understand your team members.

Getting to know everyone involved personally is even more important in virtual teams than in local teams. Be open to people.

As we have already discussed, trust plays a central role. An essential prerequisite for building trust is openness. For Bernd, Linda is "some African" with relationships in the London financial world. He is suspicious and shows little openness to get to know Linda more closely. Because of this mistrust, Bernd challenges Linda's proposals. He does not want to give her control.

Bernd also protects himself against getting to know the others personally. He wants to see his parameters defined, and to have the knowledge that everything is running as he thinks is best. The opposite way would be better: by getting to know the other person, confidence and trust would be built and security in the relationship would automatically follow. If you understand how a person thinks and feels, then you understand even better how they will approach their tasks.

Discover the Strengths of the Individual Team Members and Leverage Upon These

Claude focuses entirely on the strengths of the team members. He is enthusiastic about what Anne, Linda, and the New York professor bring to the table. Bernd, on the other hand, focuses on the deficiencies, on the problems that have not yet been solved, and he believes that he himself must come up with the solutions.

I have always a big fan of a strength-oriented management. If I encourage my team members to use their strengths to solve problems, they succeed in managing the problems on their own. What are the strengths of your team members? To find this out, you do not have to rely solely on your gut feeling. There are scientifically sound methods which you can incorporate into your work, for example the "StrengthsFinder" of the Gallup Organization.

The StrengthsFinder 2.0 tests 34 different strengths. Some examples of these strengths are strategic thinking, empathy, and self-assurance. For each team member, the five greatest strengths *In addition to simple question techniques, there are scientifically sound methods to determine the strengths of people.* can be determined. With this information, you can then develop a plan for how these individual strengths can be used for the betterment of the team.

As a manager, however, I also like to work with relatively simple methods. For example, team members can ask each other about their strengths. This works both in a workshop environment as well as online. Here, for example, are some key questions to ask:

- What is easy to do in your job?
- What gives you energy and joy in your work?
- What is your biggest success so far?
- What do people ask you to help them with?
- With whom do you often work? If I ask him/her – what are your strengths, what would he/she say?
- What do you think is your biggest strength?

In the end the person asking the question may add his perspective "I think your biggest strength is ..."

The strengths discovered through this and other methods serve to define further roles and responsibilities. When you have discovered the real strengths of a team member, you can give them tasks that they find fun and fulfilling. Instead of constantly checking the clock or complaining, they will be motivated to get the job done. This topic will be addressed more completely in Chapter 5.

Offer a Clear and Structured Communication from the Start

Virtual teams have a plethora of communication channels: phone, e-mail, Skype or FaceTime, the Cisco and WebEx tools for video conferencing, closed online discussion groups, and more. These options for communication are not in themselves problematic, but how they are used may well be.

Often, virtual teams come together on very short notice when a problem arises. These conference calls are certainly necessary, but they are not enough if you want your team to be truly successful. It is not enough to have quarterly meetings to inform the team members of their progress. With quarterly updates, the team leaders tend to present the team with lots of data, which seems irrelevant and distracting for the team members' individual work plans.

One of the deciding factors as to how successful a team will be is how clear, concise, and structured communication is from the start! With Bernd, he is doing *Have you ever been bored during a telephone conference? Communication over long distance is often poorly organized and ineffective.* quite a bit right here. While he is letting himself get too stressed, Claude is always making fun of him to help him relax. On the conference calls, Claude gives the team members plenty of talk time and makes them responsible for their part in the project.

It is important at the beginning that everyone has a say and has enough speaking time. Bernd still has to learn two important things:

1. Constructive debates should be encouraged. When the crowdfunding discussion arose, Bernd wanted to discuss the specifics with Linda and then make his own decision. It would be best, however, to discuss the matter with the entire team and then decide. In some cases, it is best to allow the team members to find their own solutions within the time and budget framework provided.

2. How the individual members of the team have developed since the last conference call, both in terms of their work and personally. Additionally, each individual needs to be given time to present a report on their progress. This reduces boredom and requires everyone to participate. Although Bernd has known Anne for a while now, he still only asks her for facts. Yet, given the circumstances of the catastrophe in her home country, he should show a genuine interest in how she is dealing with a difficult situation in a country shattered by disaster. For example, what does it mean for Anne's own children now that their mother is almost completely occupied with crisis management?

As the head of a virtual team, you should begin to build and strengthen personal relationships. Team members will not get bored or distracted during a conference call if the conversation varies between more formal, structured conversations about the project and a genuine personal interest in how each team member is doing. On the contrary, they will look forward to sharing and giving everything they can.

The second part of this book, chapters 6 through 8, is devoted to the topic of communication. There we will focus on the communication channels, frequency and structure of communication in virtual power teams.

Recognize and Reward Exceptional Performance

What motivates people to excel and to give their best varies from person to person. Bernd, for example, dreams of the possibility of people's being able to laugh in a land haunted by a catastrophe. This would be a completely new and very memorable experience for him, since he has never worked on something like it before. At the same time, he is under great pressure to make this project an economic success, a fact which he does not openly admit to his team.

Meanwhile, Claude wants to have fun, and yet at the same time, he wants to shine with a success story in the international professional world. Anne first fulfills her duty to her country and her government. Linda is fascinated by the project. As an African she can identify very well with the problems of the affected people. She wants to help. What can be an attractive reward for each of these different people?

I know a lot of managers from virtual teams who simply assume that their people will get involved and give their full performance. After all, they are getting paid for it, and they get to collaborate with other experts on a very interesting project.

The reward offered should match the performance achieved and be very attractive for as many as possible in the team. Otherwise, it does not make any sense.

In my experience, people want to be heroes. They want to rise above themselves in a meaningful way on a winning team. I have experienced absolute miracles when people have come together to work for the fulfillment of a dream. Money can play a role, but it should not be the only reward you should think of. For example, a wonderful common experience can also be a reward. A meeting with a prominent personality or attending an event that your team would otherwise not have access to could be possible rewards.

Two things are important: first, the reward should match the commitment you expect. You cannot expect a maximum performance and promise a reward that is "nothing special" for some of the team. Second, the type of reward should include all team members. People-oriented team members, for example, want to end up with a community experience and not just money. Idealists want to see and feel that they have changed the world a bit. Here the circle closes to the first success factor: the better you know your people personally, the easier it is for you to provide the right incentive.

Three Tips for Team Rewards and Recognition:
1. The boss can offer a very generous reward for the team if they manage to finish the project much faster than planned. After all, the costs saved by finishing early will cover those of the reward.

2. Let your team know about the rewards far enough in advance, preferably at least six months beforehand. You need more time for a virtual team to realize and be motivated by such rewards.

3. Why not let the team itself decide what the reward should be? Organize a brainstorming event and let the team vote on the rewards. In this way, you will know that the reward is the right reward for this team.

Combine the Four Success Factors!

You have now been given four success factors, which right from the beginning will ensure that you can unite top people from all over the world to your virtual power team:

1. Relate to Each Other on a Personal Level

2. Discover the Strengths of the Individual Team Members and Leverage Upon These

3. Offer a Clear and Structured Communication from the Start

4. Recognize and Reward Exceptional Performance

These four factors are closely related. The key to all of them is looking at your people, their differences, and their personalities. The better you know your team members, the better they feel about their role in the group and the better you recognize their individual strengths and needs. You can now communicate in such a way that everyone understands the main goal or vision of the project and their individual role in accomplishing it. They feel as if you are treating them like a valuable partner rather than some anonymous number, and they can set their individual goals accordingly. In addition, you will also learn what motivates your team and how you can reward them for their outstanding performance. With these, you are able to encourage and empower each individual team member to bring their unique talents to the table.

Chapter 3

It Is Easy to Lead When Everyone Has a Goal and Is Allowed to Shine

Bernd shook hands with his construction manager and headed for the waiting taxi. After all the problems, his project in Frankfurt was finally back on track. While he was walking along the dirt road, he checked his e-mail on his iPhone. A new message from Anne caught his eye. The subject line read: *Good news*. Hesitantly, he opened the e-mail to read it.

Not watching where he was going, he almost ran into a concrete mixer, which had just entered the building site. With a loud honk, the truck driver jolted Bernd back to the present. He stepped aside and stood on the empty wooden pallet which was lying in the mud next to the construction site and signaled the taxi driver to wait a moment. While the truck drove by, he read Anne's mail.

Anne wrote: *The government has accepted our offer. The state of Transmontania will pay 50% of the costs we have declared. The remaining 50 percent will have to be financed through crowdfunding.*

"Yes!" This was the breakthrough Bernd had long dreamed of. At last he would be an international entrepreneur. Overcome with joy, he made a fist and pushed it high into the air. "We did it!" A warm, strong energy flowed from his chest throughout his whole body. "Let's get this done!" he thought, as he walked over and got in the taxi.

As they drove along the highway to the airport, Bernd watched the skyline of Frankfurt go by. He was euphoric. It felt like something really big had begun to take shape. He contemplated how he would share the news with his team, how he would coordinate the local construction workers in the building of earthquake-resistant houses, how the proposed designs tens of thousand of students would look, how they would manage the crowdfunding, and so much more. And *he* was boss of all of this! At this last thought, he felt a bit queasy. Suppressing his feelings he said to the taxi driver: "Can we drive any faster? The fast lane is free." The driver gave no answer. Silently, he blinked to the left and accelerated.

Once he arrived at the Frankfurt airport, Bernd went to Starbucks for a coffee. He sat down, took out his iPad, logged onto the free WiFi, and began to write an e-mail to the team. His tone was almost enthusiastic. After he briefed them on all the new information, he invited them to a telephone conference for the following Wednesday.

Bernd is euphoric, because the project has finally started. He sees himself in the fast lane, but the financing is only halfway covered. Plus, there are a lot of technical problems with Skype.

This time, Bernd had lunch before the conference. Relaxed, he put his feet up in his office and clicked on the green button to start the Skype conference. Claude, Anne and Linda could hardly wait to report what they had achieved. The MOOC had begun. Anne had met with the head of local construction workers, and Linda was done with the description for crowdfunding. All she needed was Bernd's okay, and the internet platform could to go online. The ball was rolling, and Bernd felt the enthusiasm of his entire team.

"Do I have a green light for the crowdfunding campaign?" Linda asked.

"Not so fast, Linda," Bernd answered. "I would like to please check the text first. And then I would like to telephone with your friends in London who will help us with the fundraising. It would be nonsense for people whom I do not know at all to participate on our financing..."

"Bernd, I beg of you," Claude interrupted, even before Linda could react. "We agreed that we want crowdfunding. So, let Linda and her team decide how to do it. I do not really see why Linda needs to introduce us to her contacts. The main thing is that she has these contacts and that they will help us get what we need."

"But it's roughly 50 percent of our funding!" protested Bernd. He took his feet off the table and sat straight up. "In the end, I am responsible for everything, and I want to see what is happening. I want to be able to intervene before something goes wrong." Bernd felt heat in his neck.

"Okay Bernd, what would you like for me to do?" Linda asked somewhat resigned. Her voice now sounded cool and distant.

"I would like to have a telephone conference with you and your contacts in London. We'll go through the whole process together." Bernd felt that something had changed. The enthusiasm had disappeared. In addition, there were technical problems. His Skype connection was interrupted time and again, and he had to re-dial to get back online. Towards the end of the conference, Bernd firmly repeated for the record the next tasks which each person agreed to do. After everyone hung up, Bernd stood up and went to the window.

Linda wants to organize the crowdfunding campaign on her own, but Bernd won't let her. He wants to have control so that he can intervene at any time. It is clear that the mood is shifting.

"Somehow, they seemed to pull back," he thought. "But we have a common plan and agreed upon actions."

A week later, Bernd sat back in his office and went through the minutes of the last telephone conference. Out of curiosity, he had logged into the MOOC the night before, and he noticed that suddenly requirements on the houses were being defined, which had not been discussed. These new requirements could only be coming from Claude.

Bernd was shocked. Did the young architect think he could simply do what he wanted? And what about Linda? She still had not made an appointment for a telephone conference with London. Bernd had not heard from her since last week. Angrily, Bernd grabbed his iPhone and clicked on Linda's mobile phone number in his address book.

"Here is the voice-mail of Linda Ogedengbe-Smith...," Linda's energetic voice resonated not even a second after he dialed. "Great! She's turned her phone off!" Bernd yelled sarcastically and threw the iPhone furiously at his desk. He got up and walked around the room. He could feel the blood rise in his neck and face.

"Now that the project is finally moving forward, they're playing games with me! Why does Claude do such things? And Linda! Why is Linda is always so strangely rebellious? Now she has gone too far. If she were here and not in Africa, I would go to her office and give her a piece of my mind..."

After Bernd calmed down, he wrote Claude a message over Skype: "Can we please talk as soon as possible?"

Early the next morning Bernd finally reached the Canadian. Bernd was at home in his narrow study. It was still dark outside. Claude was sitting on the sofa in his open, minimalist dwelling in Montreal. The TV could be heard in the background.

Bernd has the impression that the team doesn't not follow his leadership. Claude tells him that his micromanagement style is detrimental to the team, and Claude again proposes a workshop with Paul.

"Claude, we've been friends for years," Bernd came to the point. "Damn it, why are you just doing what you want to do without telling me?"

"Listen, Bernd," Claude said quietly and calmly. "I am putting my reputation as an architect on the line for this project. I am ready to get deeply involved. But when it comes to architecture, I cannot be limited by what you tell me to do. I can't even listen to the students alone, as great as the MOOC is. I have to pass quality standards here. Do you understand that? I work on the project one day a week and have no time to spend on amateur ideas."

"Alright. Let's discuss what you need and want in detail another time. I've got a more pressing question. Do you know what's going on with Linda? I have not heard from her for a week. I have no idea how the crowdfunding is going."

"I spoke with Linda briefly. Look, she's activating her own hard-won network for you, and yet you want to explore the process and waste her contacts' time and energy. It is quite clear that Linda is angry. Come on Bernd, this is another game – you are leading a global team of top experts, and you need to trust your team. They present their plans; you can ask as many questions as you like but try to avoid giving specific advice how they should do it."

"Time is running out. How can we get them back on track?" Bernd asked. "What was the name of your guru mentor?"

"Paul."

"What advice would he give right now?"

Claude answered a little cynically, "I think you know the answer to that. He would advise doing a workshop together. It's the most effective way. At the workshop, we would establish our goals and roadmaps. And we would get the full commitment of each and every team member to reach these goals."

"Claude, would you please make a budget estimate including Paul's fee, our travel, and how much such a workshop would cost?"

Claude: "Will do, Buddy. Glad you are asking."

It was now 8:30 in the morning on May 21st, and the light of dawn gently bathed the blossoming cherry trees. Bernd stood in the conference room of the hotel "Le Meridien" and looked out over the glittering water of Alster Lake. He was gathering his thoughts before the start of the first face-to-face workshop with his team.

The night before he had had dinner with Paul. Paul was a quiet guy with graying hair who looked straight into your eyes while conversing, radiating calm and serenity. He was a good listener who, every now and then, asked sharp, provocative questions.

Bernd felt a bit nervous, but after having met him, he knew that he could trust Paul. Bernd also felt relieved that he could just observe and participate today but did not have to moderate or be in charge. Everyone except Anne would be present. She would be attending by video-conference. As a government crisis commissioner, she could not justify a trip to Europe at the moment. Besides that, her little daughter had become ill. Paul had assured Bernd that the workshop would work in this hybrid format as well. In these workshops with international teams, it would always happen that individual participants could only partici-pate by videoconferencing.

Meanwhile, the team had said good-bye to Skype. Claude had long been work-ing with WebEx, a profes-sional Cisco software. He told Bernd the advantages of WebEx, and Bernd bought the annual license for the team. With WebEx, the team had a lot more possibilities to watch files together or to use a whiteboard remotely. In addition, the connection would finally be sta-ble. "Today we get to see how stable WebEx is," Bernd thought as he checked the big screen on the wall on which he could see the conference room in Transmontania where Anne would arrive at any moment.

Paul runs a hybrid workshop for the team. During the work-shop, some of the team members are present in the room; one is connected long distance. Instead of using Skype, the team is now using a more professional solu-tion called WebEx.

Through the open glass door, Bernd heard Claude's and Linda's laughter. As soon as the two of them arrived the workshop could begin. 9:00 a.m. on the dot.

Bernd welcomed everyone first. "I am looking forward to this unique opportunity to meet all of you personally. And I would also like to welcome Anne, who is coming to us via our new WebEx system."

Then Paul took over. "I know you are all experienced experts in your fields," the mentor began.

"Today, we are going to turn this All Star group of individuals into a real working team – a stellar constellation; a strong team built with a strong foundation, despite the geographical distances between us."

After opening with a dramatic personal story of his own, Paul moved to the team's personal introductions. Everyone was asked to draw and explain his or her personal and professional lifelines on a flip chart. People began sharing the moments of which they were most proud as well the most difficult ones they'd managed to overcome.

Linda told of a shocking event that happened while she was studying in London. She had just found a part-time job at a bank in the city when she learned that her father had been killed in a bomb attack in Nigeria. She gave up her job, completed part of her studies in the long distance learning program, and went back to Nigeria to help out her family during this difficult time. As she spoke, Linda had tears in her eyes.

After Linda was done, Paul asked the others what they considered Linda's greatest personal strength. Everyone agreed that it was her resilience.

Claude told how he had won a soapbox race as a child. He had been the only boy to construct and build his own racing car all by himself. All the other boys had been helped by their fathers. At an early age, Claude had already demonstrated and developed his talent to construct things, to compete in competitions, and to achieve high goals.

Bernd was amazed. Although he had known Claude for years, he hadn't known his story. Bernd realized that he has a team of fantastic individuals, each of them shining in their uniqueness and brilliance like stars. Knowing what they had come through helped Bernd let go and trust them much more.

After this exercise, Bernd felt closer to his team, especially to Linda. She had mastered such difficult times! No wonder she could have little understanding for Bernd's impatience and distrust.

Paul continued with an exercise in which every team member would discover his greatest strengths. For this, the team worked in pairs answering simple, clear questions, which Paul provided. At the end of the exercise and observing objectively from the outside, the entire team decided what the greatest strength of each team member was. After that, it was time to work on team goals.

Paul divided the team in two groups and asked them to ask each other questions about the project. Some of the questions, for example, were: What can you just not let go of? What is your gut feeling telling you? What inspires you? These cleverly chosen questions brought to light many unspoken things. The ambition and competitiveness of each individual team *By sharing their professional and personal "Lifelines" with each other, the team bonds at a personal level. With Paul, the team establishes the three most important topics. "Being able to work independently" is at the top.* member became as clear as their individual visions for the project.

In the next step, they considered the problems and chances of the project rather soberly and analytically. In the third step, all three participants worked together to create a picture which showed what the team's greatest possible success would look like.

Finally, the three most important issues for the team were chosen. Everyone had three votes.

Bernd was not surprised that "being able to work independently" was chosen as the most important issue for his team. What Bernd didn't expect and, what really positively surprised him, was how much knowledge, wisdom, and life experience of all his team members had. He first only realized this this morning. Bernd was now determined to give his team more independence and personal responsibility. He was just not sure how to do it.

Paul continued with the workshop: "Let us now transfer our three most important topics into goals according to the SMART formula."

Managing a Team Remotely:
Using Personal Strengths and Individual Goals to Succeed

Bernd survived his first leadership crisis. His team was not following his instructions – Claude was going his own way, and Linda was not doing what was asked and didn't provide any feedback.

In real teams in one physical location, these scenarios are not as likely. The boss can always visit his team in their offices and set things straight. In virtual teams, however, such situations are quite common, particularly if the boss tries to micromanage or is autocratic. What exactly has led to this crisis?

Bernd was used to deciding everything himself. He told his people both what they should do and how they should do it. In his German construction projects, this style of leadership has always worked well. Even with his current project in Frankfurt, Bernd solves problems by everyone what to do. He relies on his experience. Until now, he has always known how to get solid financing, reliable partners, and good architects.

In his first international project with a virtual team, Bernd is suddenly overwhelmed with so many uncertainties. It makes him nervous not to be able to see what individual team members are doing for days on end. This lack of control is why he responds with an authoritarian style of micromanagement. Unfortunately, however, this does not work. Claude runs off and makes his own decisions and Linda refuses to talk to him.

In virtual teams, management crises may occur faster than in classic teams. The geographical distance makes managers feel less secure and may increase their desire for more control. Instead of micromanagement, it is important for the team to establish common goals.

Bernd's psychological motive for this behavior is fear. He fears something will go wrong. He believes that he alone will be responsible for the project's success or failure. To feel more secure, Bernd tries to control the entire process. He interferes in the implementation of individual tasks and wants to determine how team members will reach their individual goals. He does not realize that he has a virtual team with experts from all over the world who know much better about their part of this project than he does.

Linda has already done a lot of crowdfunding projects. Bernd is a newcomer in the field but still wants to have a say, simply because he is the boss. No one knows more about their architectural needs than Claude, but Bernd has to add his own two cents.

If you want to unite the best in a virtual power team, the first step is *to define and to focus on a common goal*, which the *team itself* has established. How each of the individual team members fulfill his or her individual objectives should be decided and acted upon by the individual team member him- or herself.

Steve Jobs

The legendary founder of the Apple Corporation, Steve Jobs, once said, "It makes no sense to hire smart people and then tell them what they have to do. We hire smart people so that they can tell us what we should do."

An authoritarian leadership style simply does not work in high-performance, virtual teams. Even if some team members are much younger and less experienced than the boss, they need a great deal of freedom to do their jobs. Also, the boss in virtual teams needs to understand that he cannot and should not micromanage the activities of his team. If, however, he gets the feedback he needs, he will have less need to control everything.

Feedback, therefore, is the most important factor in the success of a virtual power team. It keeps the teams alive, informed, and gives them their power! The main job of the team leader is to regularly ask for feedback and always keep the communication channels open so that the individual team members can give feedback. If a team member suddenly does not give any more feedback, like in Linda's case, then something is wrong.

Only in the case of a crisis or a massive conflict can the head of a virtual team be more authoritarian than usual. Even then, do not be arbitrary or intimidating. In this case, however, there should be a clearly defined process in which the boss first gets feedback from each individual team member on the problem and then works with the entire team to find a way to get

The virtual team leader should only bring his authority into play in crises and in conflict situations. This should occur, however, only in very specific circumstances. The rest of the time, he should be more of an "enabler" empowering his team to move forward.

back on track. Then, each team member should recommit to the team and the team's goals.

Most of the time, the boss in a virtual team has more of an empowering role. He encourages his team and makes things happen. The only aspect in which he is the absolute authority is in communicating the "why" of a project - the mission and the great goal of the team. This is the core of the energy that attracts everyone on the team and ensures that they stay actively and enthusiastically engaged.

When the Team Leader Needs Coaching

Bernd was frustrated because his team either failed to follow his instructions or to give him sufficient feedback. In a virtual team, there are many ways to hide. Individual team members can be very skilled when it comes to not letting anyone know that they are not working or doing what they want. If they no longer answer the phone or only answer e-mails selectively, then they are hiding. This behavior frustrates both the colleagues and the boss.

This frustration typically leads the team leader to intervene and to begin to micromanage. This, in turn, further aggravates the conflict and can even completely demotivate individual team members. In the worst-case scenario, this frustration is so great that the team leader becomes burnt-out, or the conflicts escalate so far that individual team members have to be let go or choose to leave the team themselves.

In both of these cases, it is the responsibility of the team leader to press the "Reset" button. In most cases it is best to get support from outside. An experienced coach can ensure that the team members communicate again, clarify their conflicts, and re-establish their commitment to the team goals.

How to Create a Positive Spiral in your Virtual Team

For many team leaders, the first impulse when faced with a difficult situation is to become more personally involved. They simply believe that there is no other option and that everything depends on them. Although this may function in a traditional situation, with virtual teams this can lead to a stand-still, because you don't have the regular contact with your team. In virtual situations it is almost impossible to affect a situation from above. It is much more important – and effective -- to discover and use the knowledge, skills, and potential of every member of your team and to find solutions together. The key to doing this is being able to activate the team's slumbering potential.

The personal abilities and life experience of each team member create the foundation for the team's mission to unfold and develop. Team leaders often make the mistake of thinking that the individual team members already know each other well, because they regularly communicate with each other about the project or because they interviewed the colleagues to bring them onto the team. This communication, however, tends to be very superficial. When the group comes together to discuss their background and their strengths, team leaders are usually very surprised to learn how little the team members know about each other. Moreover, because the team not only speaks about their strengths but also about their lifelines and what has shaped them throughout their personal and professional lives, they learn what is truly important to each team member and what motivates them in their innermost heart.

I described this method in chapter 1. In my experience, every time I have held such a workshop I have been astounded by the talents and hidden potential found in each team member. In every single group with which I have worked, we have discovered amazing talents and experiences. Trust that this will also happen with your group. As your team members discover the impressive experiences and talents of each of their colleagues, they will trust each other more and grow together as a strong entity. Then, when a difficult situation arises, you (and the others) will know who on your team can solve it. You, yourself, will not need to become personally involved or feel that you have do the work yourself.

Discovering these individual strengths is the key to launching an upward spiral. In Chapter 2, you learned about science-based methods, such as the StrengthsFinder 2.0 from Gallup. You also learned some simple ways your team members can coach each other

In virtual teams, it is almost impossible to have any effect from above. The key to success lies in the ability to activate each individual's hidden potential. Every person has more in them than they initially show!

with targeted questions. With these questions, your team members determine each other's strengths and ambitions within an hour or so.

Once you have done these exercises with your team, it is important to visualize the results. This is best done by drawing a map of your team's resources ("Map of Resources") on a metaplan wall or on a whiteboard. List all the names of your team members and write down the main strengths for each of them. In doing so, you should map both the team members' own assessment of themselves as well as the assessment of the other colleagues on the team. Such a map has a very strong effect. Each team member can show publically which accomplishments they are proud of without hiding or trying to be modest, and the entire group can see how many strengths and accomplishments the team has all together. This visualization shows the group how strong they are and how much potential they have. It also shows if there are any areas in which they need to bring in additional team members to support the group. With this exercise, the group clearly sees that they have the talent and resources that they need to reach their goal.

Method:
In a group, draw a "Map of Resources" of your Virtual Power Team. Do this by writing on a white board or on a Metaplan board all of the names of your team members and each of their strengths. This helps you and your team to visualize the true potential of your team. It's also really motivating!

How to Determine Your Team's Three Most Important Issues

Once the resources of the group have been visualized, it is important to determine the three most important issues facing your team at this moment. We choose only three issues, because three is an easy number to track the progress on. We do not want to overwhelm your team with an endless list of potentially unimportant or irrelevant topics.

I would like to take a moment to look in more detail at the proven method that Paul used with Bernd's team to determine the three most important issues. When I use this method with my clients, I divide the teams into three groups. Occasionally, as in Bernd's case, the team is too small for three groups, so the team works in pairs. In this situation, they work in pairs for the first two steps and then come together as a group to work on the third step. When I work with larger core teams, I divide the team into three groups and give each group the following assignments:

Group 1:
The first group is given the assignment to explore possible issues from the subconscious, more implicit level. The group is asked to focus

on everyday situations with the project, which are never discussed or spoken about. We draw a human silhouette on a flip chart and write the following open questions on and around it, which helps the group become consciously aware of subconscious thoughts and desires.

Questions to Activate Subconscious Thought:
When you think about the everyday project situation. . .
. . . what comes to mind? What do you think about? (Head)
. . . what is your heart's desire? (Chest)
. . . what is your gut feeling? (Stomach)
. . . what are you itching to get done? (Hands)
. . . what is causing you feel weighed down as if you had chains on your feet? (Feet)
. . . what would help you take flight or get off to a running start?

Each member of the group is asked to write down his or her perspective individually. There is no need at this point to discuss the answers or to reach a consensus. This exercise is simply about collecting thoughts and ideas.

Group 2:
The second group is given the assignment to put together more factual, explicit information about the project. They are asked to write the current challenges and opportunities of the virtual team, which seem obvious to everyone. Because this group actually addresses problems that the group is facing, there is usually a tendency to discuss them. These discussions should be kept to a minimum. Again, this exercise is not about finding solutions but about collecting ideas and different perspectives of the project.

Group 3:
The third group is given the assignment to create a visual representation of the virtual team's unusual and outstanding success. This exercise should challenge the group to be as creative as possible. For

There are some interesting and effective group exercises to help have everyone – introverts and extroverts – participate in deciding what the team's three main topics are.

this exercise, I give as few instructions as possible, so that the group is as free to explore and fantasize about their creation as possible. There is no right or wrong way to do this.

I am always amazed and surprised to see what ideas people come up with when doing this exercise. They draw real pieces of art on white boards and flip charts, or they discover unusual, creative metaphors for the success of the team.

Bringing It Together:

Once all three groups are ready, the team comes back together again to share their results with each other. The members of the first group are asked to share their notes and observations with the team. The others may ask questions for clarification if necessary. With this part of the exercise, it is important that everyone has a chance to speak. Note that some of the more introverted team members may not want to say anything at all. If you let this happen, some very important, insightful observations may go unmentioned. They should also share their thoughts with the team.

After the first group is finished sharing their insights, one or two representatives from the second group should present their group's results to the team. Again here, other team members should be encouraged to ask questions for clarification or to asked how these ideas were reached. Then, a representative from the third group stands up to present the picture they drew. Often the work of art speaks for itself and needs no explanation. Sometimes it may be necessary to explain parts of the drawing.

Once all three groups have presented their results and everything has been clarified, it is time for the group to vote on which three issues are the most important to the team. Each team member gets three votes and is encouraged to cast these votes by marking the three topics that they feel are most important with a marker.

The moment of truth comes after all of the votes are counted. The three topics with the most votes are the topics on which the team will focus. Each time that a team does this exercise and the top three topics are revealed, something very important happens at the psychological level: The team develops a strong feeling of connection. They bond together. The beauty of this exercise is three-fold. First, the top themes are not defined by the boss. This sets a strong, clear signal of respect and interest. Secondly, everyone has an equal say in the results, and last but not least, we've collected both conscious, rational input as well as subconscious, more instinctive input. In a simple and democratic way, the team was able to look at both and decide together which topics were most relevant.

Once the three most important topics are established, it is time to convert them into goals according to the SMART formula. I am sure that the SMART formula from project management is certainly familiar to you. As a reminder, SMART is the acronym for

Specific
Measurable
Attainable
Relevant
Timely

A goal is defined as "smart" only if it meets these five conditions.

The SMART formula has proven itself to set clear, measurable and verifiable goals.

The Greatest Hurdles when Defining SMART Goals

There are, of course, times in which people on a virtual team don't think about the others on the team or the common goals of the team; they focus on themselves. Every member of the team has their own personal ambitions and goals – some of which they have not even shared with anyone else. This is normal. These personal ambitions and goals are known as **Hidden Agendas**. If these hidden agendas, however, are not in line with or begin to conflict with the team's goals, problems arise, and they can sabotage the entire process.

Hidden agendas can be very diverse. They can be related to career or professional goals. They can be related to personal or relationship goals. They become harmful to the functioning of the team when they are in conflict with the team or its goals, *The three most important development areas of the team are converted into goals according to the SMART formula. Be careful! Hidden agendas, micromanagement and know-how often cause unexpected challenges.* and the transition from harmless to harmful hidden agendas, or intrigue, is fluid. For example, if one team member tries to get more recognition in the team or if a team member tries to extract money for personal purposes, trust is broken, and the team is in danger of falling apart. It is often difficult to recognize the destruction until it is too late.

The best way to overcome destructive hidden agendas is to assure that a transparent target goal process is in place in which regular feedback occurs. Also, allow team members to speak openly about their personal and professional interests, while making sure that each team member has clear goals that correspond to the team's goals. It is for precisely this reason that we involve all team members in doing both the strengths exercise and the exercise to determine the three most important topics for the team. The strengths exercise helps you as team leader to get to know the team members better, so that you can begin to anticipate possible hidden agendas. The top three topics exercise allows all team members to participate and give input as to the direction and goals of the team. Because everyone is involved in the process, everyone owns the results. As you work with your team, it is important that you give praise only for the accomplishment of team goals, not individual goals. This reminds the team of its focus. If no goals have as of yet been reached, praise all behavior that promotes cooperation and cohesion within the team.

The second greatest hurdle in virtual teams is one that we have already discussed in detail: micromanaging. Even if all of the team members have committed themselves to the team and its goals, the boss can destroy the team's motivation and therefore hinder the team's ability to reach its goals through excessive control and micromanaging. I cannot emphasize enough how important this point is. No matter how great an expert and how experienced the team leader is, their purpose is to remind the team of its mission, not to get involved in the details of each team member's responsibilities. The only exception to this is when a team member asks for the team leader's input or advice.

In addition to hidden agendas and micromanagement, there is a third major hurdle on the way to reaching your team's goals. These are the **critics and know-it-alls** on the team. They always find something to criticize. How do you ensure that these critics do not block or de-motivate the other team members? The best way to do this is to have clear goals and to give positive feedback each time the team makes progress towards its goals. This positive feedback from the boss reassures team members that they are on the right track, and it overshadows any negative criticism that they may have received from the critics.

Virtual teams easily bring top performance to the project once the potential of each team has been established. Working independently is easy once each individual team member is clear about their goals and mission.

This being said, there are cases in which the critics and the know-it-alls just have to find fault with something. They simply can't let it go. If you find yourself in this situation, speak to the critics and try to figure out their motivation for being so negative. Speak openly and forthrightly to them about their behavior and explain how the negativity hurts the morale of the team. Work with them to find other ways for them to express their concerns if the concerns are about genuine problems. You may find as team leader that you actually have to intervene while the critic or know-it-all is criticizing something or someone and call them on this behavior.

Fortunately, I have had very few problems with critics on the virtual teams I have led in the past. By carefully selecting your team members, letting them work responsibly on their own, and giving recognition at key moments, you can help otherwise very critical people to offer valuable, but limited, constructive criticism. Once again, if you want to lead your virtual team to achieve top results with ease, they need three things: 1) the knowledge that you know and respect their talents, experiences, and unique potential, 2) for you to set clear goals for each individual as well as for the team as a whole, and 3) for you to give everyone the opportunity to work independently and be personally responsible for their results. If you do these three things, you will be successful.

Chapter 4

When goals are interlinked,
Each Team Member is Accountable

The workshop was in full steam.

As the morning sun spread its powerful rays across Hamburg, bathing the hotel conference room at "Le Meridien" with bright streaks of light, Paul took off his jacket and rolled up his sleeves. He knew the workshop was going into the decisive phase. Claude and Linda were standing in front of a flipchart. They were speaking loudly and gesticulating energetically. They were one of two groups of two working on key issues for the team. Every few minutes, everything got quiet. Then, Linda would write a new idea on the flipchart.

Bernd sat at a table in front of his open laptop. He was also fully engaged in conversation, although he was speaking in a much calmer fashion. He looked alternately at Anne on the screen with WebEx and *Paul continues with the workshop for the team. The team members work on the crucial themes of "empowerment" and "integration of external resources."* then back to his computer. The two of them posted their ideas on a virtual whiteboard.

Paul stood quietly, watching everyone from the back of the room. Every now and then he would go quietly to one of the groups to make a suggestion or ask a question. As a facilitator, his job was not to give answers but to help them come up with their own ideas and solutions.

Claude and Linda worked on the subject of "empowerment." The two discussed what they would feel and experience if the goal of maximum self-responsibility had already been achieved. Claude was once more reminded of how important this subject was to him. His excitement showed. Bernd worked with Anne via WebEx on the topic of "Integration of External Parties." They were working on the question of how the construction workers, the government, and the professor from New York could best be incorporated into the team.

After a short while, all four of them were ready to report on their results and to share their conclusions, goals, and roadmaps with the other group. Claude and Linda began.

"I want absolute freedom," Claude said loudly and clearly. Bernd had to smile. "This is Claude," he thought. The Canadian stood by the flipchart, and Linda stood next to him ready to interject her thoughts at any time.

"This means I can make decisions without first checking with Bernd." Claude continued; "As long as I remain within the budget and the timeline is not affected by my decisions, I should be free to do my work unsupervised. If each of us acts responsibly on our own, we will be able to check our progress on our weekly phone calls. Each of us can report what we did during the past week. If problems arise, they don't have to be solved by the entire team; the person responsible for that area should be responsible to come up with the necessary solutions for the problems. If that person needs additional assistance, they should contact only the specific team members necessary to find that solution."

Linda nodded in agreement. She hated it when others wanted to unload their problems on her without thinking about a solution.

"Bernd, you can ask questions or give advice," continued Claude, giving Bernd a friendly look. "But the operative decision for each individual goal should be made by the immediate person responsible. If I need your help in prioritizing or negotiating with external parties, I'll come to you."

Everyone nodded approvingly. Next, Bernd and Anne presented the SMART goals that they had worked out. This was followed by the others asking questions and giving feedback. Bernd kept a protocol of the feedback given.

Then Paul asked everyone to get up and get ready for the roadmap exercise. Claude and Linda went into their corner of the room and Bernd moved nearer to the video screen. They had just started to define milestones when Anne raised her voice over the video conferencing sound system.

"I'm so sorry to interrupt. Even though my primary role is participating in our meeting, I am also required to check for anything urgent coming in on e-mail. Just now an e-mail arrived from our local construction companies. They are sharing the results of a new cost estimate, and state that they will need about 25 percent more budget than initially requested, due to a new detailed plan using the results of the new MOOC design."

"What ?!" Bernd screamed. He hit the table with his fist and jumped up from his chair.

Linda remained unmoved. She watched Bernd's reaction, then said with calm consideration, "I'm afraid we cannot

A Sudden Shock: Anne gets an e-mail that the government wants 25% more money. The project no longer seems financially feasible.

finance this additional cost by expanding our crowdfunding campaign. You are already aware that the campaign is stagnating. We found only a few investors. People have participated in small numbers, and with small amounts, and there is no more coverage coming in via the media to strengthen our push for this funding."

"What, damn it, is going on?" Bernd shouted. He was so angry that he had not even heard Linda. "This endangers our entire project!"

"Unless you build more efficiently and thus more cost-effectively" came the calm voice of Paul from the back corner of the room. Everyone turned to Paul. "I have experienced larger and more negative surprises than this one. What I see here before me is a team of top experts who are beginning to trust each other. I'm sure you'll find a way. There must be someone in this world that can do this for a lower cost."

After the coffee break, Bernd was still upset. He realized that they would need to find some help, and with this caliber of team members, a solution would be found. He was becoming timidly optimistic.

Drawing the group back together, Paul said "I suggest that we continue with the first two roadmaps and then work as a whole team on a third new roadmap that is about cost-efficient construction!"

Shortly thereafter, Claude and Linda were standing in the middle of the room writing every milestone on a metaplan card and laying the cards on the floor. Today's date and the end date of the project were marked, allowing team members to lay the cards along the timeline and walk back and forth between them. This enabled them to test the points of the timeline to see if the task written on the card was the right task at the right time and if the order of the cards was accurate.

As everyone began slowing down, lunch was announced. Anne timed out for an hour, ate a little, and went looking for her daughter.

Following lunch, Paul gathered the group together and said they would now go into the next round of the roadmap exercise using the timeline Linda and Claude had worked on. "Let's work on this example: Empowerment."

Paul was in a position so that everyone could see him well, including Anne on VTC. "Imagine, today is the day when you have fully achieved your goal."

He asked Linda and Claude to stand on the spot on the floor that marked the end point. "At this moment, all team members have acted independently and self-reliably. They feel fully empowered!"

For the next round of the workshop, Paul asks everyone to imagine what it would be like if the team had already fully achieved its goal.

Paul looked around. Everyone nodded. "So, what are you missing from the perspective of the goal? Be spontaneous. Write down what you think."

Paul moved over to the screen where Anne and Bernd were working on the topic of "integrating external parties." He looked at the digital whiteboard and asked the two to imagine they had successfully integrated all external partners.

Paul asked, "Now that you have achieved this milestone, what advice would you give to today's team that is just beginning to integrate the external parties?"

Anne immediately had an idea: "Bernd, let's name an ambassador for every key party we are dealing with. This includes the external parties. We will invite the ambassadors to the monthly telephone conference. In turn, our ambassadors will take part in the most critical meetings of the external parties and will have a brief moment to speak when appropriate."

Bernd nodded approvingly. Claude overheard Anne's comment and started listening with great interest.

"I'm sure there are others like Claude who would be delighted to be the liason," Anne added. "That person would provide information about the state of progress but would also provide information on issues which affect the respective organizations." After everyone had briefly added their opinion, the topic "ambassador" was added to the whiteboard.

Paul then announced the last round and asked both teams to present their roadmaps. Each team had to decide among themselves who would take responsibility for which of the intermediate objectives. The other group would ask questions, make suggestions and, if necessary, even challenge the decisions. Paul also encouraged everyone to actively intervene for certain interim goals when that person believed they had the necessary and perhaps more relevant personal strengths to achieve it.

There were heated discussions, and Bernd went so far as to describe some of Claude's ideas of empowerment as "nonsense." Bernd still seemed to want as much control as possible. Finally, however, he gave in. He began to realize that in future he would have much more time for overview of the essentials, and he could provide support on a more senior level.

Claude, Linda, and Anne did their best to make Bernd's role as a senior adviser seem appealing, and Linda and Claude gladly volunteered to be ambassadors. At the end, Linda and Claude held up several cards with the goals for which they were immediately responsible. Anne and Bernd had marked their goals on the whiteboard.

Paul explained that soon everyone would realize that these goals of the individual team members were interconnected with each other. "Imagine the individual targets intertwining like gears. No one person can achieve his or her goal without others reaching their goals."

Paul advised Bernd to remain largely free from operational targets, because he needed to be available to the team at all times as a guide and supporter.

Then Paul said, "Now, let us all tackle the issue of how to build more efficiently and cost-effectively."

After the last round, each team member is then responsible for setting several intermediate goals. The groups have to agree on who will be responsible for each goal.

Everyone in the core team is responsible for one of the most important team goals: articulating their vision. Teams in corporations often fix their vision in writing. Very often, these are three or four sentences in typical manager jargon, which don't trigger any emotions and with which the team members cannot identify.

As leader of a virtual team, you have two options to make it better. You can be charismatic and stand before your team like Martin Luther King: "I have a dream," painting your vision vividly and passionately, reaching your employees through their emotions. Or, you let the team work out their vision themselves. In most cases, this is the better alternative. In this so-called "bottom-up" approach, there are simple coaching techniques to guide you and your team. While doing this exercise, it is important to be creative, to stay focused on the targets, and to address all of the five sensory channels.

In virtual teams, it does not work if several people are responsible for one goal. Each team member should be assigned on large goal for which they are responsible.

Once the vision is clear, it should be broken down into annual targets. One huge difference between local and virtual teams is that, in local teams, the vision can be translated into three or four major strategic goals, and several people from the team can be designated to be responsible for tracking these goals.

In my experience with virtual teams, however, having several people responsible for a common goal has never worked well. It works much more efficiently when the vision of the virtual team is broken down into many individual annual goals. Then everyone on the core team can take responsibility for a single goal.

Method:
   Together with the core team members, or Leadership Team, define the most important team goals. Do this in such a way, that each core team member is responsible for exactly one of these team goals. This ensures that each core team member carries the same high responsibility as every other core team member. Through this, they own the project.

Virtual teams need intermediate targets and one member of the core team should be responsible for each goal. The core team, known as the "Leadership Team," consists of those who report directly to team chief. Everyone decides together, however, how to achieve the goals within the prescribed time and budget framework. All of the members of the core team are responsible to achieve their goals, and as a result, when they reach their goals they get the credit and the glory.

Avoid the Propensity to Hide in Virtual Teams

Have you ever worked really hard on a project, and it seemed like other team members were not nearly as motivated as you were? This is much more common in virtual teams than in local teams. In a virtual team, it's possible to ignore phone calls or not answer e-mails. This ends up frustrating and angering other team members. The result of such behavior is that the productivity of the team will drop rapidly. A virtual environment opens up a lot of possibilities to hide, and often, no one is able to control what each team member is doing.

Let me tell you about my own personal experience. I love sports, especially track and field. At age 40, I started to compete again. I don't know if it was a mid-life crisis, or whether it was due to one of my daughters saying, "Papa, you're getting older." At any rate, I returned to competitive sports, and I soon was the Bulgarian master in spear throwing and discus throw. In addition, I won the Balkan Championship in 2014, which includes competitors from 18 nations. One year later, I was second in the European Masters Games in the discus throw.

I am not writing about this to brag. It drives home, rather, my point of how much performance dominates my approach. Performance is my most important motivator. For my personality type, performance plays a much more important role than power or money might for someone else. Can you imagine how frustrated I was when I was working at my peak performance level on my team while other team members were shirking their responsibilities and commitments? I learned a lot about leading virtual teams from these experiences. As a result, when I lead a virtual team, I break down the team goal into many individual goals, and each core member can take responsibility for one of these goals. If everyone has their goal and has to deliver results for this goal, no one can hide.

Each Employee on a Virtual Team Needs Clear Goals

As we have discussed before, micromanagement does not work in virtual teams. Even in local teams, micromanagement reduces productivity. In virtual teams, such intervention is completely counterproductive. Team members of virtual teams need full freedom and self-responsibility to achieve their goals. This freedom and self-responsibility is what is meant by "empowerment."

The core team members should define their goals in such a way that they match the personal strengths of each team member.

Members in virtual teams are separated by time zones and cultural differences but are linked by technology; therefore, they need freedom to align their performance with clearly defined goals. Here is where the importance of clarity is manifested. How do you define goals for individual team members to match personal strengths? When the boss assigns the goals, enthusiasm and real commitment are missing. Team members should choose their own goals in a synchronous process. What do I mean by "synchronous"?

In virtual teams, there are two types of collaboration: synchronous and asynchronous. That is, either all or a majority of team members work together at the same time, (synchronous) or the collaboration over time in a series of events (asynchronous). Examples of synchronous collaboration are presence meetings and all types of video or telephone conferences, with live interaction among team members. Asynchronous collaboration takes place via e-mail, chat programs or the electronic exchange of documents. This is where each individual member of the team decides when they will react and when they will complete a task.

The defining of objectives requires synchronous collaboration. If the team members are to agree on common goals, it must be live and interactive, because it depends on the whole person, their potential and their ideas. The best format for working out objectives is in a workshop. Here, the team can brainstorm, debate, and discuss, allowing each team member to defend their opinions and positions directly with the other team members.

Bottom-Up Goal-Setting: With Roadmaps It Works Well

When it comes to setting goals of a virtual team in a group, it is rarely a good idea to exclusively refer back to existing goals. This should be obvious, but if the team leader tries to lead from the top down, this reliance on preexisting goals inevitably happens. If the team leader sets the goals and communicates them "from the top," the team members usually cannot identify with them. Of course, it is important that the team goals match the goals of the entire company. Each virtual team, however, needs to consider a lot of things that are not applicable to the whole company: the specific mix of people, the unique problems in their day-to-day business, expressed or unexpressed problems, dreams, individual concerns, and so on.

Be Careful of this Trap!

Team members have a difficult time identifying with goals which are determined from "above," from the organization or from the boss. They identify well with goals that they themselves have established.

In Chapter 3 we enumerated the three things to consider for the definition of goals according to the SMART formula:

First, individual desires, worries and emotions. Second, the opportunities and problems for the entire team. Third, a picture or symbol that serves to identify the success of the team. This "bottom-up" approach, combined with a democratic process in deciding which issues are most important, ensures a much greater commitment when everyone gets on board.

If you have defined the three most important goals for the virtual team according to the SMART formula, then these three goals summarize the team's success. This provides the basis for developing roadmaps. Roadmaps, in turn, are the series of the many intermediate objectives necessary to achieve these three major goals.

As Paul showed Bernd's team during the workshop, there are four steps to creating effective roadmaps. The team works in three groups. Each group adopts one of the most important objectives defined by the SMART formula.

I recommend the "Timeline" technique using moderation cards to mark the timeline and each step on the timeline on the floor. We call these floor or room anchors. This method is from NLP, and it activates the subconscious mind. It is important to activate the sub-

Four major steps lead to a roadmap in a workshop. I recommend the "Timeline" technique, because it activates the subconscious which helps create a stronger commitment from each team member.

conscious, because in doing so, you enhance thought processes, and you help the participant to free up the conscious mind to be more creative. Workshops are the ideal place to do this. In the teams with which I have worked, the timeline exercise has often led to new and surprising ideas. In addition, this exercise helps you get a deeper and more loyal commitment from your team members.

The Four Steps to a Roadmap with the Timeline Technique

A timeline is simply an imaginary line on the ground that symbolizes a time axis. For example, if you're working in virtual mode, paint the timeline on a digital whiteboard. If the participants are in the same room, they can position themselves at different points of the timeline and distribute floor anchors along the time axis using moderation cards.

Timeline Exercise:

Step 1: Here and now. The team members decide where on the timeline "Today" or "Here and Now" is, and they lay down a moderation card with the word, "Today" or "Here and Now" on it. From the perspective point of "Today," the participants describe the goal. In describing the goal, two things are very important: 1) the goal should be concretely and positively expressed in the present tense (i.e., "We remain focused and reach 10,000 new customers." Not, "We will not let the competition distract us and take away our customers.") and 2) define the goal according to the SMART formula with all the associated criteria, measures, involved parties, etc. This exercise does not work abstractly. On the contrary, the participants make a journey through time in their minds and should be completely transformed into the state that will reign when the goal is reached. Everyone should associate an image with the goal they want to accomplish, and they should have an emotional attachment to this goal.

Step 2: Achieved goal. The group now walks along the timeline to the end point, where the target goal has now been reached. Everyone imagines what this is like and asks themselves now that our goal is reached, what events have occurred? Ask the team members to express what they are experiencing with all their senses. What do they feel? What do they see? What do they hear? Taste? Smell? Then ask what have we missed? What have we possibly overlooked? The team looks back from the perspective it's success to the starting point, the "Today" card. What advice would the successful team give itself, if it could speak to the team members at the point where it started with the project? All of these notes are written down.

Step 3: Setting intermediate targets. The events that were mentioned in step 2 each get a moderation card, and these cards are laid down on the timeline roughly at the points when these targets need to be realized. Once these initial intermediate targets are laid down, the team should stand on each target looking back at "Today" and ask if there are any other targets we need to consider to get to this point. Once the team is certain that all of the necessary targets have been placed on the timeline, proceed to step 4.

Step 4: Responsibility for intermediate targets. Everyone now looks at the intermediate targets and milestones which have been thus far recorded. Who will take responsibility for which intermediate destination? The team then decides which specific team member will be responsible for each intermediary goal. The criterion for this decision should not only be connected to their functional role in the project. More important is the individual strengths of each person. These strengths should be the primary deciding factor in distributing the responsibilities for the goals.

Step 5: Integration. Each of the three groups has now worked on one of the three goals defined by the SMART formula, and using the Timeline technique. Through this exercise, each group has agreed on the intermediate goals and who will take responsibility for them. These results are presented by each group to the other two groups. Members of the other groups give feedback. That is, they debate both the intermediate goals as well as the decision of who will be responsible for each intermediate goal. This brings together the collective wisdom of the entire team and it allows the entire team to be responsible for the decisions made.

The outcome of the workshop is that it provides answers to the questions of *what* to do, *how* to do it, and *who* does it. The goals defined according to the SMART formula are the *what*. The roadmap using the timeline exercise determines the *how*. And distributing responsibility for each of the intermediate goals determines the *who*. This method produces two important results: First, a clearly defined plan is decided upon at a very high level. Second, team members are motivated, and they now know what they will be responsible for.

Empowerment and Cultural Differences

Empowerment plays a central role in virtual teams. Empowerment means empowering people to act independently, transferring responsibility solely to them.

Through many years of experience, I know virtual teams work best when all team members have as much autonomy as possible. In practice, this means developing topics "from bottom to top," equating the team members with the boss and strengthening self-initiative at all levels. In many Western countries, such as Germany, Great Britain, the Netherlands, or Scandinavia, this autonomy mirrors today's current culture and the prevailing values. This approach, however, contradicts the culture and values in many Eastern countries, such as Russia, China and Japan. How does these cultural differences impact the style of work in international and multicultural teams? How do team members from authoritarian or hierarchical cultures react and work on virtual teams, where leadership is autonomous for each member of the team, and each person is empowered to make their own decisions?

To shed some light on this matter, I refer to the work of Erin Meyer and her book *The Cultural Map*. The author distinguishes the cultures of the world according to a total of eight key dimensions. Empowerment is the key to the eight dimensions. In an extreme case, one team member may be from a culture that is entirely authoritarian while another is from a culture with an egalitarian style of leadership. In a purely authoritarian culture, for example, in Russia, power and decision-making are exclusively in the hands of the boss. The employee must accept decisions from above completely and without question.

In a very egalitarian culture, for example, in Sweden, all the members of a team are equal. Each team member can start initiatives and make their own decisions independently, as long as they stay within set boundaries.

Team members from authoritarian cultures will slowly accept democratic leadership. If you have patience and empathy, these transitions go very well.

In my experience, it is much easier to lead people from an authoritarian culture into an egalitarian leadership style than to convince people from an egalitarian culture to accept authoritarianism. Those who have not experienced democratic structures can get used to them relatively quickly. In turn, team members who are already accustomed to a democratic approach will never accept authoritarian power. If you do it right, you can lead teams of Europeans, Asians and Africans, and no one country of origin or style of leadership will dominate. I have led many such teams, and in all of these teams, I was successful with a markedly egalitarian leadership style.

When your team of mixed cultures comes together the very first time, it is important and essential to announce the rules of leadership immediately. This should be done in a synchronous team format, preferably a workshop. After you have all explained how the leadership will work, you should apply your leadership style consistently and demonstratively from that point on. Everyone should communicate regularly and on an equal footing with everyone else. In these regular communications, everyone should receive feedback, praise their own initiatives, and empower team members to make their own decisions within the set framework. You will observe that the team culture begins to superimpose over the respective cultural background of individual team members. The longer the team works together, the more homogenous the team becomes. Individual cultural characteristics disappear, and the team begins to create its own cultural dynamic.

How to Successfully Integrate Team Members from very Authoritarian Cultures

You may find that team members from very authoritarian cultures need additional support to get accustomed to egalitarian and democratic ways of working together. It may take some extra encouragement here and there to help them make their own decisions and solve problems independently, instead of relying on you for the answers. I have had the most success with my teams when I have been consistent in my attitude, have had patience with individual team members, and have given them the courage they needed to work independently. There are some cultures, Russians and Chinese in particular, where you should expect the process to take a little longer and to have a somewhat flatter learning curve. In workshops and other synchronous formats, it is important to treat all cultures with equal respect. It also helps to highlight the advantages of authoritarian cultures.

When necessary, be flexible and plan to give a little more guidance at the beginning to team members from authoritarian cultures. This is, of course, more challenging than it would be leading a team of more homogenous colleagues. You will find is that with people from more authoritarian cultures, you can create very disciplined and committed teams that are quick to act without lengthy discussions. Under certain circumstances this is a great advantage. Nevertheless, I always recommend an egalitarian leadership style for multicultural virtual teams.

Method:
Treat all cultures with respect. Recognize that each culture, no matter how different or how authoritarian, have strengths that may help your team. One strength from authoritarian cultures is, for example, discipline. You will need to give more instructions to team members from authoritarian cultures at first. It doesn't take too long, though, until they begin to adjust to a more democratic style of leadership.

Some time ago, I worked for a customer who exported everyday consumer goods to Russia and was suddenly confronted with new, very strict market regulations. As a reaction, the company had to completely change its marketing strategy for Russia, in comparison to their Western markets. It was very difficult in Russia to define turnover targets, because the state made it increasingly difficult for Western companies. Russian culture is very authoritarian, so the company held their first meeting with its Russian top managers alone. The managers discussed the problem and prepared a first draft for the new strategy on the Russian market.

It is a break-through experience for people from authoritarian cultures or from less developed economic situations to purposely discover and apply their personal strengths and talents.

The company initially brought me in to lead a team workshop with their middle management, working with those who were responsible for one single business unit. When we were doing the exercise to the personal Lifeline, the participants were amazed at how little they knew about colleagues with whom they had been working for years. The employees discovered their own personal strengths, worked out the three most important topics, defined goals according to the SMART formula, and finally created their roadmaps. When the top managers saw the results, they were positively surprised. They realized that there was once again valuable input for the new strategy, which very closely matched the market. They were also amazed at how much commitment to the new strategies had developed in just one day. One top manager spoke of this exercise as providing a "breakthrough" for companies with challenging market conditions.

What Interlinked Goals Can Achieve

If you work out the three most important topics of the team, define goals from the SMART formula, and create roadmaps based on these objectives, where all team members assume responsibility for intermediate goals, then in the end all goals connect together like a set of gears in a machine. Through this system of "interlinked goals," you ensure a high commitment of all team members, and you prevent individual team members from hiding and not contributing. The more responsibility a single team member owns to reach his or her goals, the better. This means additional collaboration, more interaction, and strengthened attractiveness of the virtual team.

The three main effects of interlinked goals:

1. **Empowerment.** All team members have their own goals and can shine when they have met them. Self-initiated, bold decisions, and action orientation are seen and valued by the others. In addition, team members have the freedom to ensure results within their defined limits. This reduces the dependency on the boss, and stimulates cooperation with other team members at the same level.

2. **Increased performance.** Each team has three groups: approximately 10-15 percent are high performers. These are the team's performers. Between 70 and 80 percent are reliable team workers. They achieve their goals and secure the basis for success. About 10-15 per cent are low performers. These low performers do not necessarily have to leave the team, but know that they will deliver less than the average, reliable team member. If the lower-performance members do not have their own strategic goals, it is very likely that they are hiding. This means, for example, that they do not reliably answer calls or e-mails.

   If, however, all the objectives are interlinked and if the less reliable members have defined goals, the achievement of which is linked with the goals of the performers, then no one can hide. As soon as all the goals are interlinked, a healthy kind of group pressure is created, which at the same time forces these weakest links to perform at the level of reliable team members. One of the biggest advantages of interlinked goals is that the boss does not have to exert any pressure on the less-reliable team members, because the group does this for him. Together the team pushes toward an increase in performance. Of course, the boss should always keep an eye on the situation and should offer help if it is needed. I will deal with this in more detail later.

3.   Gravity. The third effect of interlinked objectives is a substantial increase in gravity, or the "gravitational force" of the team. Interlinked goals ensure that the individual team members have to communicate and work together more intensively. Since everyone is in some way dependent on everyone else to achieve their goals, the team's cohesion increases enormously.

You have seen in this chapter how to develop shared goals in workshops with your virtual team, and the results of these interlinked goals for the team as a whole. I have always been surprised at how well this method works with my teams. If this is done correctly, individual team members will not be able to hide. The performance of the entire team will increase, because low performance members will be forced through peer pressure to improve their performance level to match those of their colleagues.

Chapter 5

When Team Roles Meet the True Strengths of the Team Member, Work is Enjoyable

Bernd felt the sweat running down his neck. He ran faster. His body felt good. He was pushing himself and his body was synchronizing perfectly in rhythm. His breathing flowed smoothly. The muscles, the joints, everything harmonized. Bernd liked to go to the gym, and he especially liked the phase at the end of endurance training when the body feels lighter and the even movements balance the mind. This evening it was particularly intense. "These must be the endorphins," thought Bernd. "No matter what, it does me good."

Suddenly, the financial problem came back in his mind. They had to build more efficiently and, ultimately, less expensive. Bernd remembered the discussion at the end of the workshop with Paul. They agreed that they had to find someone who had already built such houses extremely cheaply. In a way, Bernd was spoiled. Money had never been an issue on all of the construction projects he had lead in Germany. Obviously, he had to present himself as being efficient and frugal in order to win contracts, and every budget he had worked with had proven to be enough money to see the project through. He had never had to reconsider or change plans in the middle of a project before.

"I guess Claude is as spoiled in Canada as I am here in Germany," thought Bernd. "We'll have to find someone else."

Bernd was seriously determined to find someone to make this work. Feeling fit and full of energy from the fitness studio, Bernd was ready to go! "A little research, several phone calls," he thought, "then I'll have someone who can build these houses cheaply." Bernd suddenly stopped right in his footsteps. Wait! I can't do this! I have a team of stars each of whom wants to shine. Why should I try to get involved again? After all, Claude is a born networker. He knows people all over the world, and he seems to enjoy finding them and staying in contact with them.

The team needs to build more efficiently and save costs. Bernd resists the temptation to find a solution on his own. Instead, he trusts the "master networker" Claude to find someone to help.

Bernd finished his workout on the treadmill. He cleaned the handles with disinfectant and set off for the shower. The shower room was empty. He turned the water on and felt the jet stream massaging his head and body. Several times he switched between hot and cold. How refreshing! He dressed and went to the front desk, where he stopped briefly to write an e-mail to Claude on his iPhone:

> *Claude, would you be willing to activate your fantastic network again for our project? We need to find someone with experience and expertise in building low-budget, high-quality, safe houses. Would you please see if you have someone in your network that might qualify? Thank you and good luck!*

Bernd finally reached home at 8 p.m. He, his wife, Wiebke, and their daughter, Lena, have lived in their simple, spacious, modern house just north of Frankfurt for over fifteen years. As usual after his workout, Bernd was famished. As soon as he opened the front door, the wonderful scent of dinner engulfed him, and he followed the scent to the dining room. The table was romantically set, and lit candles cast shadows on the walls. Wiebke greeted him with a kiss, and they sat down to eat.

One week later, just before one o'clock in the morning, Bernd was sitting in his office waiting to begin a telephone conference with the team. As always, he had made an agenda and sent it to everyone. WebEx, the new web conferencing tool, was much more stable than Skype. Bernd opened the program five minutes before the meeting was to begin.

The light and clear voice of Anne came first.

"Good afternoon, Bernd. How are you?"

"Oh, thank you, Anne. I'm fine. It is nice that you are always so punctual. How are you?"

"I'm fine. My little daughter has recovered from the flu. In the meantime, I have also had some talks with the government. They are waiting to hear from us about the budget adjustment. Did I understand correctly that we will be joined today by someone who can help us with this?"

"Hi folks!" This was the confident voice of Linda calling in from Africa. Bernd looked at the clock. It was 12.58 clock. They would be able to start on time.

"A hearty bonjour from sunny Montreal!" Claude was there too.

"Hello and welcome, everybody," Bernd cheerfully began. "As you can see on the agenda, our main focus today is how we will build the houses for cost-effectively. Thanks to Claude, we have been able to get in contact with an internationally award-winning Brazilian architect. She has built houses for the people in the favelas of São Paulo made of recycled materials. Her name is Pilar Ruiz, and she seems interested in joining the team. I am curious about whether her know-how can be transferred to our project. This is what we will discuss with her today. Claude, is Pilar ready join the conference?"

Pilar, an award-winning Brazilian architect, joins the team. In the Favelas, she built houses made of recycled materials. She certainly will have ideas and suggestions for the project.

"Yes, she's on standby and can join us at any time," Claude said.

"Okay, then please bring her in!" After a beep, Pilar was there.

"Good morning, good evening, wherever you are, ladies and gentlemen," Pilar said.

"May I call you Pilar?" Bernd asked.

"Please do!"

"We're glad you're on board, Pilar. Would you please introduce yourself?"

"With pleasure. My name is Pilar Ruiz. I am an architect, a city planner and an expert on housing construction. My home country is Brazil. I studied in the USA and worked for several years in Lisbon. Since I have been back in São Paulo, I have been working on several innovative projects. I was immediately fascinated by your project when Claude explained it to me on the phone. I would very much like to participate. It is a matter of heart to help the people of Transmontania after this terrible catastrophe."

"Thank you, Pilar," Bernd said. "I've got a question for you: What was your most important project so far? "

"I don't have to think about that for long! This was the favela project, for which we also received the sustainability award in Davos. We rebuilt a complete district in a very poor section of São Paulo with small houses made of recycled materials. And at minimal cost. For many of the children there, this was the first time that they had a roof over their heads. The houses contain everything a family needs to live. It's not luxurious, but it's not nothing."

"Wow, great!" Linda said. "We're glad you're joining us."

The solution proposed by Pilar allows the team to react immediately. Linda reminds Claude that Pilar is new and may need some guidance. She offers to take Pilar under her wings and explain everything necessary about the team and the project to her.

"Well, you are aware of our problem," Bernd said soberly. "What do you suggest?"

"I've looked through the MOOC plans, and there are quite a few possibilities. It's quite possible to build the houses using other materials without compromising the designs. We should discuss this with the professors who have organized the MOOC. In addition, we should involve local builders in the process, so that the solution fits their traditions. Would it be possible to form a small virtual team where we can discuss these ideas and where I can explain my experiences in further detail?"

"That sounds good. Claude, can you please take the lead? You have the contact to the university in New York anyway. And, Anne, can you involve the local builders? "

"I'll discuss it directly with the professor," said Claude. "This could mean more time for me than I originally agreed to, Bernd, but that's not so bad. We are sailing in unknown waters. I am looking forward to the solution we will find together with Pilar in our expanded team."

"Thank you Claude," said Bernd.

"It is a pity," added Claude, "that we cannot use our original plans, because they were awesome! I am sure our houses would have dusted the first prize at the world exhibition for architecture in the "Smart Designs" category. But - c'est la vie."

"We're working with some really great people here, Claude!" Linda interrupted. "Yes, exhibitions and glittering awards are nice, but we should keep our goal in mind. Our goal is to help thousands of homeless people get a roof over their heads before winter comes."

"Yes, you are absolutely right," said Bernd. "We will keep our eye on the prize. You can count on it."

"Excuse me," Claude interrupted. "I just wrote an e-mail to the professor, and he agrees."

"You know my attitude to multitasking during team meetings, Claude," Bernd said in a slightly reproachful tone. "But I'm glad the professor is on board. Thank you."

"Sorry, may I suggest something?" Linda asked. "Since Pilar is joining our team and doesn't really know us yet, I would be glad to meet with her alone to explain who we all are, what each of us does, and what we've accomplished so far. I could also show how she can access the individual documents online."

"That's a very good idea, Linda," Bernd said. "Thank you for volunteering."

"I would appreciate that, Linda," Pilar said, relieved.

"Let us set up a time this week to talk. And if you have any questions beforehand, just call me or write me a text message."

"I'm making an appointment for the new workgroup," Claude said. "Pilar, the professor, and the builders from Transmontania should talk to each other next week."

"Looks like we have a plan," Bernd said, smiling. This was the first conference at which Bernd had little to talk about. Nevertheless, the ball rolled. The project made great progress. All the team members were bright and ready to take the initiative.

Bernd noticed that he had less and less to do. The team members were working independently and absolutely reliably. They were willing to take the initiative and find solutions themselves when challenges arose. It is a wonderful feeling.

Nonetheless, Bernd felt like he ought to be doing more. He thought about why he had started this project. It was going to be the international breakthrough for him. In addition, he was going to be the savior for those in need, those who were traumatized and homeless in Asia. Now the team did the most work without him. And yet for the first time in a long time, Bernd felt like his life had a meaning and purpose greater than anything he had ever known. And he knew that this was only the beginning. For the first time, he felt a sense of being part of something greater than himself. It was more than his previous successes. It was even more than mere disaster relief. There was something new, something exciting, and he and his team were right in the middle.

Working with Ease and Pleasure in the "Flow Corridor"

In virtual teams, people predominantly work alone. They rarely, if ever, see the other team members. Because of this, the ability to motivate oneself becomes one of the most decisive success factors. So, what motivates people regardless of where they live or what they do? They want to have fun! They want to enjoy what they do. The light feelings of joy, happiness, and fulfillment are universal and not bound to any culture.

And when do we feel joy, happiness, and fulfillment? We usually feel joy, happiness and fulfillment when we do something that uses our personal strengths and that fits to our personal value system. When we work on something that interests us, uses our talents, and fits to our value system, we come into the so-called state of flow. Flow means that our tasks and our abilities fit together perfectly.

You may already be familiar with the flow theory. It goes back to the Hungarian American psychologist and fortune teller Mihály Csíkszentmihályi -- a name which cannot be pronounced correctly outside of Hungary, but this is not really so important. The decisive point in Mihály Csíkszentmihályi's theory is the so-called "flow corridor".

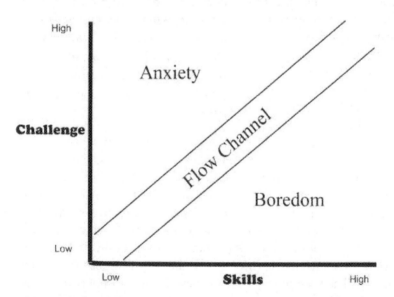

Illustration 3: The "Flow Corridor" from psychologist Mihály Csíkszentmihályi is the middle between anxiety and boredom. It is the state in which a person finds their task to be both pleasurable and motivating.

The "flow corridor" is an ideal state somewhere between challenge and overburden. In this state, we find the task that we are working on fulfilling, and while we are working on this task, we are in our center. We are focused, energized and committed. We enjoy doing this activity.

Flow Means to be Completely and Positively Absorbed by the Task at Hand.

If the required activity is too difficult or if there is too much pressure, a team member may become overstretched, frightened, frustrated, and unable to perform the task. If, however, the reverse situation is true, the team member becomes bored, unfocused and distracted. The optimal flow, the "flow" as Mihály Csíkszentmihályi describe it, is the area where the requirements of the given activity fit together with the skills, talents, and interests of the team member.

The best way to help your team members to excel and work independently is to help them come into this state of flow; and the best way to help them come into this state of flow is to know their true strengths and interests. By knowing this and helping them to take on tasks that fit their skills, you help them to be fulfilled. They will enjoy their work and feel light and energized as they work on your project. They will be willing to go above and beyond to give their best.

Methods to Discover the Strengths of Team Members

As I mentioned in Chapter 2, there are unique digital tools to help you discover the strengths of employees. One such tool is the Gallup Strength Finder 2.0. With the Gallup Strength Finder, you will be able to discover the five greatest strengths of each team member and then develop an action plan to better use these strengths in the work process. This is a very comprehensive approach. There are, however, simpler techniques for discovering these strengths. Some of them are also amazingly precise and can trigger a motivational thrust for your team members.

In my time as a manager, I often asked every team member to write down their greatest strengths in a plain Word document. For those who have difficulty identifying and describing their own strengths, there are some simple coaching questions which you can use to help them find their strengths. You can also ask your team to work in pairs, either live or online. The two team members can then ask each other questions such as these:

- What do you find easy to do in your job?
- What gives you energy and fun?
- What event in your past do you consider to be your greatest success?
- When do people come to you and ask for help?
- With whom do you often work together?
- If you asked colleagues about your greatest strengths, what would they say?
- What do you consider to be your greatest strength?

At the end of a questionnaire the respective questioner can also express his own opinion: "After all that you have answered, I believe your greatest strength is ..."

These guided self-reflection exercises always bring new insights and are often a direct energy boost for team members. The energy is created by more awareness and by the strengths of others being seen. At the end of this coaching exercise, you and the team know the greatest strengths from the internal perspective, from the point of the interviewees themselves, and also from the external view, namely as assessments of the questioners. This results in a "map of resources," which should be made available to all team members, so that everyone knows the strengths of their team colleagues. Through this exercise, the awareness that everyone on the team is uniquely gifted grows. The map of the strengths can and should be used as the guide for any decision about which persons take over which responsibilities. In addition, this exercise gives the team transparency. No one has to wonder why another team member was given preference for any given position. This can be seen from the strength profiles.

Method:
Go through the exercises mentioned to determine the individual strengths of your team members, and then put together a "Map of Resources," which your team may access at all times. This will help the team members get to know each other better, and it will provide them with an excellent resource if they need extra support.

How to Use Natural Strengths to Distribute Additional Roles

In each team, the team members can be divided into three large groups. In the first group, you have the team members who have a wide range of skills. They see the big picture and understand how things are related and influenced. If you have subdivided your customer base by geographic region, these **Generalists** are ideal for keeping connections with key figures in the respective regions. Generalists have an open ear for new needs for products and services and report them back to the team. Generalists are necessary in all teams that have direct contact with the end customer or as an internal service provider for employees in the company. An example of the latter are IT departments. They are an internal department which serves internal customers, namely, the employees of the corporation.

Of course, there are also entire departments in companies whose job it is to be in customer contact, for example, sales and marketing. Nevertheless, you can divide the internal and external customers from each team and assign them to the generalists. In this way, you promote the gravitational force both within the team itself and with customers.

The second group consists of experts or **Specialists** who have a great deal of expertise in a specific field. These people are champions in their field of expertise. Before a new product is delivered to the customer or a service is provided, the specialists should give feedback and possibly make suggestions for improvement.

In each team there are Generalists, Specialists and Team Players. If you know who belongs to which group, you can distribute roles accordingly.

This quality assurance is often not their real role in the company, but an additional task. The additional role is derived from their strengths and abilities in their particular area of specialization. When specialists give feedback, it gives the virtual team an additional opportunity to touch base about the project and the product. This, in turn, strengthens the interactions of the team and its gravitational force. It helps the team to further overcome the geographical distances.

The third large group consists of people who have a very good sense of the needs of other people and who contribute much to the positive atmosphere of the team. These are the **Team Players**. As an additional

task, team players gladly look after new team members, just as Linda did
with Pilar. They are ideal to organize trips or parties, and in doing so,
they strengthen the cohesion of the team.

When I explain in my seminars that team members are to take on
additional roles and other tasks, the first reaction is always the same:
"We are all already 150% full! How can we possibly do even more?"
In practice, however, it looks completely different. If the team members
have discovered their true strengths, then they actually enjoy taking on
new activities. People who are enjoying themselves don't look at the
clock. For many, being in the flow ensures that they actually do not
experience the extra task as being work.

The Positive Effect Additional Roles based on Strengths will have on Your Team

When team members take on additional roles on the basis of their
strengths, it has three positive effects: First, everyone has more fun,
because what they find easy and rewarding to do is fun. Second, those
taking on additional tasks get more recognition from the rest of the team.
Each team member is seen by the others with their individual strengths,
which gives the team a motivational thrust. This motivation is particularly important when people work alone. Third, there are additional
interactions between the team members, which cause more intense
bonding for the virtual team. Generalists, specialists and team players
all contribute, each in their own way to the cohesion of the team as they
take on additional roles.

Taking on additional roles have three main effects: more fun at work, more recognition for each individual and more interaction. The team continues to bond and grow.

One of my clients was a
globally active consumer goods
manufacturer. The corporation
had recently established a new IT
Project Delivery Unit for all internal projects. It was essentially
a pool of project managers that
were assigned to different business projects throughout Europe,
and they were expected to operate as a single internal business unit.
This unit consisted essentially of a pool of 30 project managers, each
of whom was at his home somewhere in Europe. In other words, it was
not only a virtual team, it was an entire virtual unit. After analyzing

the strengths of each of the team members, we found out who the generalists, the specialists and the team players are. Although all of them worked equally as project managers and were constantly involved in the project business, each of them voluntarily took over additional roles according to their strengths. The prospect of recognition made it easy to take on further roles and identify with them.

We gave four generalists the responsibility for four large geographic regions, according to the management units from a group perspective. The generalists established intensive relations with the local representatives, recognized the need for new projects, communicated them to the entire department, and developed problem solutions. The specialists were "champions" either in ERP (enterprise resource planning), in CRM (customer relationship management), or in IT infrastructure. They regularly gave feedback on individual project plans, business cases, and so on. They thereby contributed a lot to improving the quality of the work. The team players finally set up a Buddy system and looked after all the new arrivals in the department as well as the freelancers who joined the team over the course of time.

After some time, this internal unit had excellent key performance indicators in all areas measured by the corporate headquarters. The financial data agreed, the customer feedback was outstanding, and the questionnaires were full of praise from employee surveys. When the division leadership compared this department's performance to that of those for North America, Asia, Africa and other regions, the Europeans were by far number one. But the best thing was that everyone felt like a team, although they were from different places and different projects. There was intensive communication and strong cohesion. This effect was mainly due to the acquisition of additional roles according to their own strengths.

Personality Profiles Help to use Strengths and Solve Problems

As an executive coach, I often work with a relatively new personality test, the Visual Questionnaire, abbreviated VIQ. The VIQ works equally well for people all over the world and cannot be manipulated because it works exclusively with images.

The test runs in such a way, that the participants always have two pictures to choose from and click on that they like better. Sounds simple - and yet highly effective. Why?

The Visual Questionnaire is a personality test that works equally well for intercultural teams, because it works with images. It is Ideal for global virtual power teams.

For most personality tests, the results depend strongly on the quality of the translation of the questions. In addition, most of the candidates in conventional tests consider what results they would like and how they would like to be evaluated. Many test questions are, to a certain extent, transparent and one can answer them approximately as one would like to be seen. This does not work with the VIQ because the connection between the images and the personality structure is not intuitive.

The VIQ is based on the type theory of the psychologists C. G. Jung and Julius Kuhl. The basic framework consists of four dimensions:

1. Introvert or Extrovert

2. Rational or Emotional (Thinking or Feeling)

3. Sensing or Intuitive

4. Judgmental or Perceiving

The first dimension (introverted or extroverted), is about how people perceive the world. Extroverted people, for example, are more playful and more interested in new experiences. The second dimension (rational or emotional) shows whether people are more logical and objective or emotionally controlled and subjective. In the third dimension (sensitive or intuitive), people differ primarily in whether they are more detailed and thorough or if they intuitively grasp the whole. Finally, the fourth dimension (judging or perceiving) shows whether someone is more long-term and unambiguous, or open, flexible, and quick to change situations.

For a virtual team, this personality test reveals many possible findings: Where does someone have special talents? Where could they improve? How do they behave in conflict situations? Are they more a leader or a loyal follower? On the Internet, you will find much more information about the VIQ. You can try out the test online and contact me or another coach who is certified for the VIQ. Here I would like to limit myself to the practical consequences of this personality test. If you have the personality structure.

Better understanding of your team members helps you solve problems faster and overall increase the efficiency and effectiveness of team collaboration.

Method:
  Use personality analyses to better determine the strengths of your team members, to learn about their develop potential, and to know how they may react in conflict situations.

According to the results of the VIQ, each team can be divided into four groups depending on their way of thinking and acting: **Visionaries, Planners, Doers and Critics.** By doing this, they consciously form groups of people with similar characteristics. These groups of similar personality traits should then exchange ideas and develop possible solutions. In my seminars, I am always surprised at how quickly and smoothly people with similar personality structures work together.

If during this exchange of ideas, a problem arises or if you need some new, creative ideas, you can get suggestions from all four groups. The four groups consider the same problem from a different perspective: the **Visionaries** look to the future and define new goals to motivate the team. The **Planners** develop a clear process to solve the problem. The **Doers** quickly decide *Depending on how people think and act, there are Visionaries, Planners, Doers and Critics. Identify the groups and use their different perspectives to strengthen your team.* who takes care of what and are usually immediately ready to get started. The **Critics**, in turn, have identified all of the risks and pitfalls and are developing strategies to avoid them.

The next step is to reassemble the four groups. Let each group present their findings and suggestions to the others. It is always amazing how different the approach of each of the four groups is. In the joint round, each team member is now confronted with three completely different views - those of the groups to which he does not belong. This is a tremendous enrichment for all. In the last step, the whole team discusses all approaches presented by the individual groups. The aim is now to integrate the proposals into an overall plan which takes account of all aspects.

The trick with this method is that the discussion just comes to an end. If you arbitrarily classify the team members into groups, where different characters meet, then you will be immediately debated and important aspects will fall under the table. In the method proposed here, with groups of similarly structured people, the group work runs very harmonically. In the end, everyone in the respective group is satisfied with their results. Only afterwards in the big round the results are controversially discussed. So there is qualified input from four different perspectives and then the synthesis. They not only ensure a good result, but also ensure that the team members do not argue all the time. When people within the team meet again and again on the same level, this also significantly increases team cohesion.

The Fuel for Management Based on Strengths

There are many different methods to help leaders recognize the individual strengths and thought styles of their team members. The key, however, to all of these methods is always the same: it is recognition. If team members are recognized for their strengths, they become excited and are willing to invest these strengths in the team. Unfortunately, most companies are not willing to recognize the strengths and talents of individual employees.

Just ask yourself: Have you already received so much recognition in your life that you do not want to ever be praised again? Probably not. And maybe you can even remember situations in which you did something special but did not receive any recognition at all.

The most frequent reason employees give for leaving their company is not lack of identification the company or its vision. Neither is it too little financial compensation. The most common reason given for leaving their job is that they cannot get along with their immediate boss. When they asked exactly what they meant by this description, they answer that their boss never gave them recognition for the work that they did. Some even say that it has been years since their boss has praised them or recognized their work. Many different studies have come to the same conclusion: Employees do not leave the company. They leave their immediate supervisors.

You cannot Praise Your Team Enough

People often think that too much praise spoils the receiver, but in my experience the opposite is true: You cannot give too much praise. Praise is especially important for virtual teams, because the daily personal contact with other team members doesn't exist. A daily smile or nod which happens automatically when a team is together doesn't happen when the team is so far apart. As the team leader, it is important to consciously allow for praise to be said at each team meeting. It should be a fixed point in your agenda.

In large virtual teams, which can be scattered all over the world, the situation can be even more aggravating. The team members work alone and rarely have contact with their supervisors. Again and again, I hear about virtual teams, where praise and recognition have fallen completely under the table. Often the team leader has even less understanding for his employees than a large corporation has for theirs.

I have always made a conscious effort to act differently with my teams. Praise is a focal point. Perhaps this comes from my experience at home: I am the father to five girls. Five. In our family, there is my beautiful wife, our five daughters, and me. Both as a father and as an international manager, I have the same secret recipe: First, praise. Second, praise. And third, praise.

What do I mean by the word "praise"? The first and foremost pre-requisite for praise is attention. Be attentive and watch every little progress your team makes. Praise every positive contribution of every single team member, even if it has not brought the project decisively further. In addition, also praise any form of good cooperation. Give recognition to everything that contributes to a positive team culture.

Because members of virtual teams rarely see each other in person, and there are few opportunities for informal talks, you should make praise a fixed program point in your meetings. I will go into more detail about this in the second part of the book.

It is important that you also praise all team members for small contributions. There are "secret heroes" in every team. "Secret heroes" are employees who are quite far down the organizational hierarchy, and yet they still make decisive contributions to the *In virtual teams, the members hardly see each other and almost never receive praise in informal conversations. Therefore, recognition should be a fixed point on the agenda in the regular team meetings.* success of a project. The performance of these secret heroes is often hardly noticed by the other team members.

One example of how I incorporated the use of secret heroes in my work is when I headed an IT team for a large corporation, which was in charge of facilities in Eastern Europe, the Middle East and Africa. As IT administrators, our job was to install radio antennas on a roof in Uzbekistan where the temperatures reached over 40° C (104° Fahren-heit) in the shade, while our employees in Moscow had to figure out how

to lay fiberglass cable in the frozen ground at temperatures below -20°
C (-4° Fahrenheit) In many virtual teams these difficult conditions go
unrecognized. The members of the IT team are often so focused on the
software that they do not realize the difficulties people on the ground are
having. A short e-mail from the top manager which simply says, "Well
done!" can work wonders in building a strong team spirit. And through
this recognition, these secret heroes, who make the project possible, feel
valued and respected. This, in turn, motivates them to continue to work
hard for the team.

What is the best way to praise and recognize your team members?
First of all, honesty and sincerity are important. Praise only what you
believe is actually worthy of recognition. Then, you should pay attention
to the language you use, so that you can express different degrees of
recognition, depending on how much your team members have achieved
and how hard they have worked. Otherwise, the praise will quickly wear
out and lose its effect.

PART II

COMMUNICATION

Chapter 6

How Technology Helps Bridge Continents and Time Zones

Bernd was feeling increasingly annoyed. He was sitting in his office, and although it was almost noon, he had to switch on the desk lamp. The grey, rainy skies outside only served to darken the office -- and his spirit.

He had wasted over a quarter of an hour on the computer, looking for the most current plans and status reports from the local Transmontanian builders. Several hits had come up after entering the term "blueprint" into the search function, but after clicking and opening all sorts of files, the right one had not yet surfaced. Instead, older versions or files with similar names had come up first. And this was not the first time he had had to deal with poor search results! After a great deal of wasted time and energy, he opened the latest version of the MOOC design and latest status report on the crowdfunding campaign.

The team had chosen Google Drive for Work as their cloud storage document management provider. Initially it seemed like the ideal solution. Google Drive worked equally well on all PCs, Macs, and mobile devices. It allowed *After three months of the project, Bernd is annoyed with the chaos when filing documents. There is a urgent need for document management. And he wants a personal assistant.* simple uploads and had convenient features that allowed multiple people access and the ability to edit the same document. But after three months, things were not looking good. All possible file presentations were on the virtual drive: Excel spreadsheets, photos and videos; everything. Originally, there had been a logical storage structure, but now so many new folders had been added that the team members stored their files in any number of possible places.

"I do not know how people manage to deal with this chaos," Bernd muttered angrily, annoyed with himself. "I will just ask Anne where the plan is; she should be able to send me the link."

Then he questioned himself. Should he call her? It was early evening where she lived. No, he decided; its best to write her an e-mail and CC all the others. We must solve this problem once and for all!

Bernd composed the e-mail with two essential points: He asked Anne for the link to the latest version of the construction plan, and he asked everyone for ideas on how to solve the problem with the file folders. He vaguely wondered if he was really asking for someone to optimize the storage structure and take care of the cloud storage going forward. First, he decided, it would be best to hear opinions from the others.

Only a few days went by before Bernd came up against the same problem again. He could not find the file he was looking for. He was further annoyed that no one had responded to his question about to how to solve the problem. I urgently need an assistant, he thought. I cannot waste my time searching for files! Bernd already had a part-time assistant who supported his projects in Germany. She was around 40, competent, friendly and very well organized. Unfortunately, her English skills were not advanced enough for an international project. I'll ask Claude, decided Bernd. He knows all sorts of people. Bernd quickly sent out a Skype message:

Hi Claude! I need URGENT assistance for tackling this filing problem. Do you know someone?

During lunch, Bernd's mobile phone pinged, and Claude's reply came on the screen:

Assistance is the right keyword. But not just for you - we all need this assistance, not only in Hamburg, but virtually, for the entire team. The best thing would be a crackerjack on the computer who could bring order to our storage structure and look after our digital tools.

At the next WebEx conference with the team, virtual assistance was at the top of Bernd's agenda. Bernd worked from home that day, and was dressed very casually. He started WebEx five minutes before the appointment. Anne and Pilar immediately connected.

"Hello Anne, Hello Pilar! What is the current weather in Transmontania, Anne? "

"It's summer. We now often have 25° to 30° C. Ideal conditions to begin construction of earthquake-proof houses. "

"How is it in Rio, Pilar?"

"Hello Bernd! Today, we have some rain for a change."

At this moment, Claude and Linda joined the conference. Everyone was ready to start on time.

Bernd asked Claude and Pilar to report on the latest changes to the blueprints. How had Pilar's know-how from her project in the favelas worked in their favor with this project?

"Ladies first," said Claude.

"First, thank you, Claude, for bringing the professor and his team back onto the team so soon. We had a very productive workshop, and were quickly able to clarify what needs to be changed to implement my ideas for greater cost-effectiveness. The professor was extremely cooperative. He immediately got to work and promised that he and a colleague would deliver the revised blueprints within three weeks."

"Pilar has very clear ideas about what needs to be changed," added Claude, and "I think we'll get there very quickly."

"Thank you, Pilar, for working so quickly," praised Bernd.

Pilar responded, "I extend my gratitude to Linda,

Pilar has quickly become involved on the project and has clear ideas about what needs to be changed in the construction plans. Claude brought the Professor from New York and his team on board. Everyone is pulling together.

who acquainted me with Anne and Claude. They both took time to bring me up to speed, and explain everything I needed to know. "

"Gladly," said Linda. "It was my pleasure."

"You've all done a great job," Bernd summed up. "I'm glad you can function so well on your own," he added, smirking.

"I have an important concern," Bernd continued. "Do you remember my e-mail from last week? I still struggle to find documents, and often I have to ask one of you for a specific link to access it. Last week, I asked if anyone could provide ideas on solving this, but I did not get an answer. It is also important to note that we have wonderful commentary in these documents. Nevertheless, I am continually getting comments by e-mail, Skype and in all possible ways, and then in the final version on Google Drive, the comments are never complete."

Bernd paused, and clearly no one seemed to want to respond.

"I've discussed this problem in detail with Claude," continued Bernd, "and I think we need a virtual assistant. Someone who can organize well and who also understands IT. We need someone to care for our systems and our storage."

Then Linda spoke up: "In one of my recent projects I worked with a young woman from Eastern Europe. Her name is Stella, and she is from Bulgaria. Stella still studies economics at University, but has already proven herself in supporting virtual teams. In our project, she was more than just a virtual assistant, she provided efficient file management and knowledge management. This increased our productivity enormously. In addition, her fees are extremely favorable. Should I contact her? "

Linda brings the young Bulgarian Stella onto the team as a virtual assistant for. Her specialty is efficient file management. And that for very little compensation.

"That sounds like a good deal," said Claude. "I have never worked with someone from Bulgaria."

"Please send me Stella's CV and fee requirements," said Bernd. "I'll arrange an interview with her."

Two days later, Bernd sat in the Lufthansa Business Lounge at Munich Airport. He had entered one of the separate work areas and where he could talk to Stella on his iPad. He had hardly pressed the green button, and she was there.

"Good morning, Mr. Schmidt. I am pleased that you are interested in my services. "Stella was in her early twenties, spoke a bit slowly and had a slight Eastern European accent. Nevertheless, she was very self-confident and assured.

"Good Morning! We're all on a first name basis in our project. Would that be okay for you? I'm Bernd."

"Yes of course. I'm Stella. "

The young woman smiled at the camera, but Bernd felt as if she was smiling directly at him. He sensed that he immediately trusted Stella. The three-second test had already been achieved. Bernd was convinced that in the first three seconds of an encounter we decide whether we would like to work with someone or not. Similar to viewing a YouTube video, when we decide if we want to continue watching after three seconds have passed.

"Stella, we turn to you because we have a storage problem," Bernd explained in a factual tone. "We have more and more files constantly being generated for this project and we are losing the overview and connecting commentary.

In their first telephone conversation, Stella convinces Bernd that she has the necessary expertise, structured approach, and independence. The self-assured young woman is also now on board.

Additionally, we are working on a deadline and have little extra time. We must be innovative and creative and build our new buildings as quickly and efficiently as possible. Potentially, there are a lot of people who can contribute to our knowledge - MOOC students, a professor and his team, the local builders and more. Over the past three months, we have generated a lot of files, and in recent times, I find it increasingly difficult to find anything that I really need or want. In addition, people working on these various teams use all possible channels - WhatsApp, Skype, Viber, and so on - to send messages, changes, and updates. I believe that we must now arrange and unify all this at once. Otherwise everyone will soon have their own idea of the project, and we will be lost."

"Bernd, Linda has mentioned that her Google Drive for Work is used as a cloud storage. How do you deal with static documents that are processed by several people at the same time? Is there always a final, coordinated version? And how do you work with dynamic content - new ideas, useful links, personal updates? "

"Quite honestly, so far we have not distinguished between these. Everything is a jumble in the cloud. "

"And who is responsible for the individual areas? Who for the design, who for building and who for the tests? "

"There are responsible persons for each aspect of the project, but we have no superordinate structure and no organizer for the whole. "

"Okay I understand. I am familiar with such challenges from other virtual teams. In fact, your problems are common. I think you can keep the static documents on Google Drive, but with a little more process and discipline. For your online discussions and personal updates, however, you need something else, for example, a closed Facebook group. I can make suggestions for this. In such a project, knowledge management is crucial. "

"That sounds good. Can you be available for our next telephone conference next week? "

"Sure, Bernd. I'll just need someone to familiarize me with the proj-ect first. Do you have someone who can do that?"

Bernd liked Stella's structured approach. Within a very short time Stella had proved her competence.

"I'll ask Linda. You already know her, and she loves doing this type of thing!"

The Combination of Technology and Human Passion

We are becoming more and more dependent on digital technology. Can you even imagine traveling by car without first programming the navigation system or looking at the route on Google Maps? Almost any kind of information is accessible via the Internet, whenever we want it. There are also more and more digital helpers that make life easier for us. It is a very small step to total networking. The "Internet of Things" is coming. What already applies to every area of our everyday life is even more applicable to global business. Digital technologies are indispens-able. An international project has long been inconceivable without the use of e-mail, web and video conferencing. Digital tools for real-time collaboration are increasingly sophisticated.

Any technology, however, is only as good as the people who use it. How can technology improve collaboration? From my point of view, there is only one answer to this question: anyone who really wants to achieve outstanding results must combine the latest technology with passion. In private life, we prefer to use digital technologies to stay in touch with friends and relatives or to read the latest news about our interests. Many people use Skype, for example, to communicate with friends around the world to learn about what is happening in their lives.

Similarly, Facebook and other social media allows us to keep in touch with many more friends and acquaintances. We use these tech-nologies privately, so we are very enthusiastic and passionate. But what does it mean in a business context to combine technology and passion? How can you encourage people to share their knowledge with others through digital technology and create a living and productive community?

In our private lives, we use digital technology enthusiastically to be in touch with people we care about. In business, we should create the same enthusiasm by combining the latest technologies with deep passion.

What is at stake here is knowledge management in its various forms. In my experience, knowledge management through digital technology is only successful if the individual participants passionately contribute their personal strengths. Knowledge management works best when you have top experts on the team who know a lot in their respective fields and are passionate about their specialty. These experts see their knowledge as a personal strength and have a natural urge to share it with others. They love to conduct discussions and help others through their skills. The head of a virtual team needs to set a good example here. By sharing his knowledge at any time via digital media, he motivates other experts on the team to do the same.

When you have the right experts on the team, enlist and encourage them to share their knowledge, then you can then create the appropriate technical environment to use this knowledge in productive ways for your business.

Which Technologies are Essential for Communication and Collaboration?

When you have team members who do not meet in the same physical office location, you need digital collaboration technology. This is true even if your core team uses the same office, but some members (occasionally or constantly) work from their home office or as freelancers who support your team selectively. What kind of technology do you need to build a strong foundation for a team over geographical distance?

Initially, e-mail and instant messenger are easy and essential. Today, both are a self-evident part of our professional and private life. It is worth taking a little effort to organize e-mail and instant messaging more efficiently than might be the norm for personal use. In this way, you can greatly increase the productivity of your team. E-mail traffic is always increasing, and includes enormous amounts of spam mail. Despite many disadvantages, e-mail remains an indispensable tool for business. As I've already described in Chapter 4, it is essential for a virtual team to agree on a timeframe in which each e-mail needs to be answered. A standard guideline is 24 hours.

Method:
Write relatively short, concise e-mails and use clear, strong subject lines, so that the recipient of your e-mail knows immediately what

the e-mail is about. Also, be very precise about the actions that you wish for the recipient to take.

Equally indispensable as e-mail today is chat, or one of the numerous forms of instant messaging, such as WhatsApp or Facebook Messenger. When team members turn off their e-mail program (including e-mail notifications) in order to focus and be creative, they are usually still accessible via chat or another instant message program. A virtual team can agree that instant messaging is only used for urgent messages, or to provide information that requires a quick and fast response. Using one single instant messaging tool, such as iMessage (if everyone uses Apple devices), WhatsApp, Facebook Messenger, Skype, Telegram, etc., for the entire team is best. A fixed response time should also be set with instant messaging. In this case 2-3 hours is the usual maximum, since it is normal to have a break from concentrated work every few hours and meetings rarely last longer than that. Some companies are also limiting instant messaging to specific times, for example stopping between 20:00 and 6:00 local time. This is to ensure sufficient recovery and downtime, since constant accessibility can also add stress and reduce productivity.

E-mails and instant messengers are now indispensable to business. Whiteboard and Workflow Tools have also gained in importance. If the team agrees on how to deal with technology, it becomes an invaluably effective tool for success.

Two other technologies that are increasingly important in business are whiteboards and collaborative workflow tools (groupware). A digital whiteboard is designed to enable the participants of a web or video conference to work on a document in real time as it is viewed by each conference participant. For interactive brainstorming, break-out groups and the like, such virtual whiteboards are ideal. There are different products available, ranging from very specialized tools like the Ricoh Whiteboard, to simple and free versions such as Google Apps for Business.

Google Apps can also be linked to Google Drive to share documents and collaborate in real-time. With tools for workflows, I do not mean the heavy-weight enterprise resource planning (ERP) systems, such as SAP, which normally represent workflows. Rather, I have my smart digital to-do apps that allow delegating certain tasks to other team members. In these apps, the entire work progress (before and after delegation) can be stored and tracked later at any time. Trello is an example of such an app. In my seminars, I am often asked which system is best suited to manage vacation times. If you do not already have a mature HR management system for your team, I recommend a simple Google Calendar.

It is sufficient in the range of functions and the flexibility to enter the vacation times of all team members and to keep an overview.

How to Choose the Right Digital Technology for Your Team

There are two basic approaches to the selection of digital tools: "Best of Breed" or "One Stop Shop." "Best of Breed" means that you are looking for the best product for all your individual requirements. "One Stop Shop" means that you choose one of the largest IT vendors, for example Microsoft, and from this vendor use all, or almost all of their products. There have been several evolutionary cycles in recent years and decades. In the early days of the software, there was often only one vendor who had the best solution for a particular need. If you could afford this often very expensive solution, that was the best option. Then came the great time of the complete providers, such as SAP. They could provide everything from a single source, which made the integration of IT much easier. If you could afford it, that was the best solution. Today the world has changed again. We are living in a time when there are millions of apps and cloud solutions and integration among these is no longer a problem. This means you can choose almost any app or program you like and integrate it into your IT landscape.

Today, a more pragmatic approach is called for. Look for the app that suits you best, but keep the number of apps you use for certain tasks as few as possible. It suffices, for example, to have an instant messenger and a video conferencing system. The less apps you use, the smoother your communication runs and the less IT support you need.

Today, you have unlimited possibilities to use apps and integrate them into your IT landscape. However, to do this effectively, keep the number of apps for individual tasks as low as possible.

In large corporations, of course, the digital strategy of the organizations as a whole is important. But for the most part, there is a certain selection of shared apps available for individual teams. I advise you to use the apps that are desired by the majority, but then periodically, for example annually, to check whether there are better solutions which have become available.

The Limits of Digital Technology

Digital technology makes it possible to bridge continents and time zones, but do they connect people effectively? Is everything possible through digital technology? Or, is there sometimes no substitute for actual personal contact? As noted in Chapter 1, effective collaboration in virtual teams requires that all team members have at least met each other one on one once. Methods recommended by me, such as the "Personal Lifeline," ensures that people meet each other and lay foundations for interpersonal relationships. Technology comes into play to maintain interpersonal relationships, but does not create them! In order to maintain the relationship, it is necessary to communicate regularly about personal events via digital channels. A personal update is just as important as project information, specialist discussions, and problem solving.

I also want to remind you, as mentioned in Chapter 1, that critical feedback in virtual teams should never be public. Only criticize a team member in an one-on-one conversation. The problem of public criticism is exacerbated when web or video conferences are recorded and archived. Imagine fielding a sharp attack on a team member during a conference. Afterwards, it may be regretted, but it cannot be undone. The criticism will come out again at all subsequent reiterations of that conference.

Digital technology makes many things possible, but not everything. Personal meetings and conversations remain important. In addition, digital communication has its own traps that require careful attention.

In general, I recommend conducting regular one-on-one discussions with all team members - not only when there is something to criticize. If a problem arises and you wait to address it during one of the next scheduled conferences, it may be too late. Therefore, always communicate on the "short wire" with individual team members. I recommend that managers of virtual teams schedule more personal conversations at least once a month with all team members who report directly to them. During this conversation, you can discuss the performance over the past four weeks. If something is not running properly, you can point it out early. As soon as a really difficult problem arises, you also intervene, but again not in a public discourse, always one-to-one. The goal is to understand the perspective of the other team member.

Virtual work is simply different; this concept must be recognized again and again.

Another important point: even the most advanced technology does not change the fact that work can sometimes be uninteresting at home. Even with my long experience in virtual teams, I still experience this. I now work a lot from home and sometimes miss the personal interaction with my team members. It may be advisable to create occasions for personal encounters to keep everyone on track.

Always try to understand how individual team members are navigating their situation of virtual collaboration. It can be, for example, that very extroverted people are demotivated because they just have to work a lot from home. Initiate conversation with your team members and find out what is going on with them.

Conclusion: Technology is an indispensable part of effective collaboration with virtual teams. However, make sure that the passion of your team members is kept alive. Also, be aware of the limits of cooperation in digital technologies. You need at least one regular individual personal meeting with each team member as well as regular one-to-one calls on the phone. The good news: There is more and more technology to choose from and the integration into the existing IT landscape is easier than ever. If you agree on clear rules, how to deal with technologies, and everyone is disciplined, then digital technology becomes a key to productivity. Digital technology can erase spatial distances and enable the best experts from all cultures all over the world to be brought together.

Interview with Thorsten Jekel

As an IT entrepreneur, consultant and book author, Thorsten Jekel specializes in business success with digital technologies. During his career, the MBA has devoted himself to the topic of intelligent use of new technologies. He has the necessary management experience to integrate business and technical issues in a holistic way. Since the market launch of the iPad, Thorsten Jekel has developed innovative business models with his Berlin company, jekel & team, around the use of the iPad. He practically accompanies large sales organizations with the introduction of iPads in field service. His book *Digital Working for Managers. Work-*

ing with new technologies efficiently, was published in 2013 by GAB-AL-Verlag. I met Thorsten Jekel at the "Stuttgart Knowledge Forum."

Who are you and what do you do? Just describe yourself!

I show companies how they can become more productive with digital-working technologies. My career started in 1988 at Nixdorf Computer. Later, I was CEO of several mid-sized companies. In 2010, I founded my own company, jekel & team. It specializes in the introduction of iPads for major sales organizations, such as Coca-Cola. I work on issues similar to topics your book examines. For example, how real and virtual teams work together productively. Or, the best way to communicate with each other, especially if employees work all over the country or even in different countries.

What are the main technologies for collaboration in virtual teams?

In my experience, one needs two types of technologies: 1) one-off technologies that make each individual team member more productive, and 2) technologies or even apps to communicate well with everyone on the team. Everyone needs software for personal information management, such as for e-mails, appointments, or tasks, for themselves. It is important to be synchronized on all devices. This can be done with Microsoft Exchange. Then, the team needs software to work and communicate with each other on, such as scheduling and sharing files. The synchronization of all data is also essential here. It must work together on the same files in a uniform structure, in order to avoid duplicates in any case. Finally, there should be real collaborative platforms where employees can share ideas and work with project plans. Here I also see multimedia tools for telephone conferences and video conferences, and the beauty is that these tools are becoming more and more cost-effective. At the beginning of my career, a video conference was still really expensive, today it is even possible via the iPad or the iPhone and a fast, mobile connection. This does not yet work in every circumstance, but it is improving all of the time, and I believe mobile connectivity is the future.

Virtual teams need technologies that make each member of the team more productive, as well as those that enable good communication amongst team members. It is important to have synchronous forms of communication.

I am currently working for a company that previously held regional meetings in offices, and now they are making these meetings more and more virtual, with mobile technology playing a key role. Tools that I like are Adobe Connect or Cisco WebEx. With WebEx, Cisco is one of the international market leaders. This application is even available as an app for the iPad. For me, however, it is important that these systems function reliably in everyday life. So, try different systems, talk to your company and ask them about their experiences.

What technologies or apps do you recommend, depending on the size of the company?

There are very different options, depending on company size and other characteristics. For small and young companies, I recommend starting with free solutions like Skype or Google Hangouts. Google Hangouts are not always public, as some believe, but can also be used in a closed mode. For small projects, simple tools such as Projectplace, Trello or Wunderlist can be used.

Wunderlist, for example, once started as a simple digital to-do list, then it was purchased by Microsoft and integrated into the Outlook Exchange environment. Microsoft has since added the smart solution of a startup for its mature world, which I find quite interesting. We often suggest a mix of the small-scale world of startup apps and the large, established applications, such as Microsoft, for the larger companies. Skype was also bought by Microsoft and Skype for Business was then integrated into Lync.

Depending on the size of the company, you need to know if your systems are scalable. Where your data is placed also plays a role. For reasons of compliance, there may be a problem in some industries, if the data is in the US. Then you need to make sure that the servers are in the European Union or even in specific countries such as Germany, Austria or Switzerland. Since I work a lot for banks and insurance companies, I often face this challenge.

Virtual Personal Assistants (VPA) are becoming more and more popular. Do you have any experience with this trend?

I love virtual personal assistants! It's been about the ten years since I read the book "The 4-Hour Week" by Timothy Ferriss. His credo is: delegate, delegate and re-delegate. If you are short of staff, you should definitely use virtual personal assistants. I can also say from experience that virtual assistants are worthwhile even if there is enough staff. That way the company workers can concentrate more on their core tasks. You should, however, carefully consider what tasks you will assign your virtual assistant. If you do everything in English with your virtual team, that is the easiest. I need many things for my work done in German. To find virtual personal assistants who are fluent in German is not so easy.

It is worth having personal virtual assistants, even if you have enough staff. The PVA allows the rest of your staff to concentrate on the things that matter.

I also work with Beach Layer. This is a company from Berlin that employs assistants from Eastern Europe, which helps keep their prices low. I used to work with GetFriday and Brickworks, two suppliers from India, which were recommended by Timothy Ferriss. GetFriday is suitable for standard tasks, while Brickworks does country studies or market analyses. When I was managing director of a fruit juice producer, we did a first country study ourselves and then presented it as a template to Brickworks. They did the same study for twelve other European markets. This is an example of how you can perform research-intensive tasks with virtual personal assistants. Another example: I have a podcast, and my virtual assistant transcripts it and makes blog posts from it. The price range is between about 4.00 US dollars an hour for virtual personal assistants from South America and up to 25.00 to 30.00 Euros an hour with providers from Germany. For assistants from India or Eastern Europe, expect to pay between 8.00 and 10.00 Euro per hour.

What can be delegated to virtual personal assistants?

In short, almost everything. I always ask what do we need permanent employees to do, and what can the virtual personal assistants do. If you have employees in your office with whom virtual assistants can discuss things in person, it makes it much easier. However, I am on the road most of the time and then I would have to send permanent employees in my absence to present things accurately as possible. In my experience, it depends on the quality of the briefing, regardless of whether you have present or virtual employees. With a bad briefing, you get bad results, with a good briefing, good results. This is the essential point, and not whether the employees are virtual or present.

I use my virtual assistant for everything that can be done over the Internet. In such a situation, the only major hurdle is if they are not a native speaker. My virtual assistant is from Romania and studied in Germany, so he is very good in written German. However, one hears his accent when he speaks, which can be a disadvantage when he makes telephone calls. Generally, VPA vendors are unfortunately not particularly well-organized when it comes to outgoing telephone calls. So, that can be somewhat problematic.

Again, everything that can be done over the Internet works great with a VPA. I use them for doing research, creating slides, writing reservations for hotels and restaurants, booking flights, and anything that can be done online in writing and with forms.

Basically, it makes sense for me to delegate everything that a person with a lower hourly rate can do, so that I can concentrate on the truly value-added activities.

Everything that can be done over the Internet can be done by virtual assistants. One exception may be telephoning, since they would need very good language skills. The deciding factor on how successful your PVAs will be is how well you explain what you expect from them.

What do I need to do to effectively use a virtual personal assistant?

The most important thing is briefing, briefing and briefing again. The second most important is the right choice and configuration of the digital technology for the cooperation with the VPA.

For example, your VPA should be able to send and receive e-mails on your behalf. They also need a platform for file exchange and collaboration on documents. Most VPA vendors have ready-made solutions, so I already have an exchange platform for files for my VPA. If the documents are not highly confidential, I also work with Dropbox. This is one of the easiest ways to exchange documents. Confidential information requires professional solutions, such as from Fabasoft, which is an Austrian provider with a very high security standard. It is also very important to be constantly synchronized on all devices. In the case of briefings, you should follow clear rules, and the reaction times should also be agreed upon. Structure increases the effectiveness of virtual personal assistants. This means above all: well-structured briefings and well-structured digital systems.

What are your experiences with virtual teams?

I have had many different experiences. We currently have a case advising a sales organization which is represented in urban regions such as Berlin, Munich and Frankfurt, but also in rural areas which are very sparsely populated and which means long distances for the field service. The challenge is that the commutes out to the rural regions are less productive. In the big cities, the teams get together for 5-10 minutes every morning and discuss everything that is coming. This means every day at most half an hour of lost time, because the field workers are already out in the field.

We have shared with the customer how we work this out for the rural regions. We are now focusing on real virtual distribution teams that are scattered all over the country and communicate with one another, for example, through Adobe Connect.

In the field, virtual sales teams can work much more efficiently than traditional teams. Working virtually with freelancers can also be very valuable.

Another example are the many freelancers with whom I collaborate, for instance, in app development. Or another example is a food service company with whom I am working on introducing iPad technology into their workplace. We have an external app developer team, we have SAP, we have a parent company, we have a mobile device management provider, we have the individual users - and all we need is to bring everyone together. This is more and more common in companies: a mixture of internal and external team members. In the past, this has always been a bit difficult, but the beauty with the new digital technologies, is that you can integrate external team members as if they were internal employees. This works really well! I believe that in future, that you will get more and more external specialists on your internal team, which will make your team a virtual team. Fortunately, it is getting easier, cheaper and faster. The result will be that the companies become much more productive.

Which of your achievements as a leader and entrepreneur are you particularly proud of?

First, I would like to say that for me, my wife and daughter are most important in my life. If I ask myself what will remain of me on this planet, then my daughter is number one. For me, leadership and management have a lot to do with what I would like to pass on to her generation. On the other hand, I have also learned a lot from her in dealing with people, which I can apply in teams.

If I restrict my comments to purely business, the biggest success was the creation of my own company, where I earned more in three years than in all my former positions as managing director. And the companies really did not pay me badly! Interesting for your book is perhaps that I have managed only through virtual power teams, which are so fast and so successful. I started as a single entrepreneur and worked for other companies.

One of my first projects was itempus. My business partner and friend Professor Jörg Knoblauch of tempus used to sell paper-based calendar systems and we brought them together into the digital world. Long ago, the trend was for people to switch to digital calendars and apps. I said, Jörg, you have good ideas and you have a customer database with 90,000 addresses for your paper-based systems. This might be something to work with. With a team of very good app developers, we packed the proven time-schedule system into an app. This has been highly successful and is selling very well at the App Store. I could never have done it alone, because I really needed a virtual team of the best specialists.

What I have done is what Professor Günter Faltin, a very exciting man, by the way, proposes in his book, *Kopf schlägt Kapital* ("The head beats capital") as "reasons with components." Today, with digital technology and virtual teams, you can start a business very cost-effectively and still have the entire infrastructure right away. If you include external partners for each project and then work with virtual personal assistants to do the administration, you are fully scalable up and down. This is also something that large companies can learn from entrepreneurs. So, I'm a little proud of the fact that I managed to succeed with these methods so quickly.

People often fear that their employees will not work when they are not being visually supervised, so the managers risk becoming micromanagers or control freaks. How did you control your employees? How have you ensured that everyone is doing their best?

I also know a lot of people who have problems with virtual teams, because they think people do not do their job. Yes, they can become micromanagers or control-freaks. This was not much of a problem for me.

In the beginning, my problem was my lack of enforceability. I'll give you an example. I worked for the Tchibo coffee service for five years and was responsible for the service for two years. My team consisted of 25 women.

I was in my late 20's, and I talked a lot with the women. I was nice, of course, and I wanted to be liked. Then I learned that it is not about being liked, but being respected. As a manager, a clear direction must be given in order to bring the best people into a team and achieve their goals.

Your management style should always be adapted to the situation. Technology cannot replace leadership; it can only support it. Leading your team only through e-mails does not work.

I am convinced today of the concept of "situational leadership" described by Ken Blanchard.

People are different, they have different needs and do different tasks on a team. Accordingly, I must adapt my leadership style. A simple example: If someone wants to learn how to ride a bicycle, they need clear instructions about what to do - no long discussions. But if someone on a team at the Tour de France wants to refine his driving style for the next section of the track, they need quite different input and they need to discuss strategy. One should therefore always consider the whole issue of leadership based on the situation, the company, and the goals.

What I am trying to demonstrate is that technological leadership cannot replace people. Technology can help me lead, but to lead people by e-mail, for example, would not work. I was once responsible for a team of field staff who worked on their own all week. I would call them once each week. I would ask how it was going and was open to questions. Nevertheless, one worker complained about the boss always calling him. We then had a group discussion, and I asked people if they wanted more or less contact with me.

You can discuss this with employees, or external partners in virtual teams, and find a solution for your team. It is good to have the entire repertoire of communication facilities, such as telephone, e-mail, instant messenger, video conferencing and so on, but you should discuss as a group, how communication will be handled and respond to individual preferences.

How did you ensure that employees are really involved in virtual teams and that the team became more than the sum of its parts?

In different ways. First, I start with believing that everyone is doing their best at the moment, even if that is not enough for the overall team goals. Maybe someone needs support from me or someone else to perform better. This is, therefore, a value-based approach in which you get to know your people, value them, and to trust that they are not doing too little.

In my opinion, trust is the key to everything. Trust is the absolute number one. The number two is being an example for your team. Team members always look at the boss, and when the boss is really engaged, they are also engaged. I have always paid attention and made sure that I expect at least as much from myself as I expect from my employees. I think it is problematic when executives say that you have to cut costs, and then they order themselves the latest 7-Series BMW. This is simply not credible, and the employees will notice the discrepancy and not believe you.

Communicating credibly and without contradictions is important. Additionally, one must remain human. For example, I once had an employee whose daughter died of cancer. I was so glad that I could really support him in this situation. Of course, no boss in this world wants an employee to have to deal with this, but if such a situation occurs, you need to respond with real humanity and empathy.

Trust is the key to everything. It is not fair to assume from the outside that someone is not pulling their weight. And, as the team leader, I have to be an example for my team. I, myself, need to act the way that I want my employees to act, and it is important that my actions don't contradict my words.

When there is bad news, it is important to communicate this clearly and unequivocally. As managing director, I had to dismiss people, and I communicated the situation very clearly, what the reasons were, and why we had to radically cut costs. I then went forward by good example and had the 7-series BMW, which I had taken over from my predecessor, demonstratively traded in for a Citroën Berlingo. Then I asked the other managers how they wanted to save in similar fashion? One who owned a large Chrysler traded it for an economic VW Passat Diesel. Our salesmen, who had only had very cheap cars, ordered something better to motivate them to more commitment, and soon the company's position rose. When, after two years, the figures were in the black we were again profitable, the leasing contract for the Berlingo ran out. I did not return to the biggest BMW, but instead ordered a VW Multivan, the compromise in the middle. This was also a signal to the employees.

How do you see the future of virtual or even boundless teams?

Virtual and boundless teams are becoming increasingly important. The world is flat.

With modern digital technology, there are more and more opportunities to form teams on an international scale. Lower labor costs in other countries, such as South America or India, play a role, but that is not the issue. It is also about using different time zones, as McKinsey has been doing for a long time. When people anywhere in the world do things over night, the next day the other members get to work with the results. Team members from different countries can also complement each other wonderfully. In India, for example, there are outstanding software developers, but they often lack structure, while Germans are very good at project management. So, it is a good addition, for example, if project management is supplied by a German partner.

I believe it is becoming increasingly important that teams work across geographical, cultural, and business boundaries. There are external specialists everywhere, and there will be a mixture of internal and external in the future. There will also be a mix of virtual and present teams. All of these things will increase productivity. The mixture makes it best.

Chapter 7

Structured Communication Means that not only the Boss talks, but Everyone Talks — about Everything

Claude's back felt stiff and hurt. He had just finished a Skype call. 2 hours and 37 minutes. Half sitting-half lying on his sofa in the living room, his iPad was lying on his lap. He still saw Maria's face and smiled longingly. He met the Spanish architect three weeks ago at a conference in Barcelona. After three romantic days with her, he remained constantly in touch - long Skype phone calls, text messages, Facebook posts, the full program. He checked his e-mails and saw the reservation confirmation for his flight to Rome next weekend. There, he would meet Maria for the second time.

"I have to find a project in Europe, otherwise the flights across the Atlantic will ruin me," Claude thought. "I cannot afford going every two weeks." Then he saw an unread e-mail from the MOOC professor which was already two days old. There were delays with the new, more efficient blueprints. This, in turn, has caused the test buildings of the local builders to be delayed. Claude should have told Bernd immediately. "I better call him instead of forwarding the e-mail," Claude said to himself out loud. Bernd will not be happy about this delay. It affects a critical thread of the project. Claude pressed the Skype button. He had the gentle voice of Maria still in his ear and didn't even notice that it had already rung ten times when Bernd finally accepted the conversation.

"Claude, do you know what time it is? In Germany, I mean!"

Claude quickly calculated that it was 1:00 am in Hamburg. "Oh Shit, Bernd, I'm sorry!"

"Why are you waking me up?"

"Sorry, Bernd, I did not think of the time difference. We have a delay in the MOOC blueprints. As a result, the test structures will also be delayed. So, the entire time schedule has changed."

"Did you just learn that? And what do you think I can do in the middle of the night to help you?"

Claude has fallen in love with a Spanish architect. Because of his long Skype calls with her, the quality of his work seems to be suffering. Bernd doesn't understand what is going on.

"Okay, right now you can't do anything. I will set up a video conference with Pilar and the MOOC professor's team to discuss how we can speed up the process and what the worst case scenario is for the timing of our project."

"Just do it, Claude. And do it as fast as possible!" Bernd was still slightly angry. "Do you need anything from me?"

"No, no, Bernd. Thanks for asking. We're fine. I'll get back to you tomorrow at the end of the day."

"Okay, then wish me a good night!"

"Sleep well, Bernd."

Claude knew how to create a sense of urgency to activate people. He immediately started writing e-mails and sending meeting requests. Nevertheless, he was disappointed in himself. The long phone calls with Maria during his usual working hours in Canada, when it was later in the evening in Europe, steered him off. He had already forgotten dates and read important e-mails too late. "I need to concentrate more on my work and somehow separate my work and private life better," he thought. Easier said than done. It was so nice to be in love.

On Wednesday the following week, Bernd prepared for the upcoming team conference. He had just finished a telephone call with his construction manager in Frankfurt. "Comically," Bernd thought, "the team in Frankfurt is robbing me of more time and energy than my international, virtual team for Transmontania." They seemed to be reaching the "empowerment" goal that they had defined together with Paul. The workshop began to pay off. Bernd was extremely satisfied with how much self-initiative the people showed. Linda had already successfully completed the crowdfunding campaign.

The money was there. Now she helped Pilar and Claude to coordinate the MOOC architects and builders. Pilar really helped the team move forward and seemed to be accepted by everyone. Anne arranged formalities

Everything is going great! Everyone in the team shows a lot of self-initiative. The money is here. Pilar helped the team decisively. Bernd's only concern is Claude.

with the government quickly and efficiently and ensured that the local builders were kept up to date. Stella, the new team member from Bulgaria, had introduced effective file management. The team members now shared a lot more online and held lively discussions in the newly founded Facebook group. The ball was rolling - and Bernd had to do little, if nothing. He did not need to control anything either. The team actually seemed to organize itself. Bernd's only concern was Claude. He has rarely given feedback lately, which was very unusual for him. For this, Claude called in the middle of the night to bring bad news. "This has got to stop," thought Bernd. "I need to discuss this with him at the conference today."

It was a crystal-clear day. The Elbe reflected the sunlight and threw interesting patterns on the walls in Bernd's office. Bernd blinked, dropped the blinds and started WebEx. It was 12:55 pm. As usual, Anne and Linda were on time.

"Hello Ladys, how are you?"

"Great, Bernd. I see that we are really making progress!" Linda added.

"I'm fine, Bernd," Anne answered quietly. "I have some news from the builders about the test buildings."

"Good. Let's wait for the others."

At 1:00 pm, everyone was at the conference except Claude.

"I suggest we start now," Bernd said. "There is plenty on the agenda today. We have made great progress since last week's conference. Pilar, thanks for your fantastic ideas! Your suggestions are now being reviewed by the architectural team in New York. I am very happy with the collaboration between the architects and the builders."

He continued, "There is, however, some bad news. Claude reported a delay in the new designs, which is critical to our timetable. As we all know, people need their houses by the winter. For some reason, Claude thought he needed to call me with this bad news in the middle of the night!"

He paused. But no one went to his remark.

"Pilar, has your joint conference with architects and builders been held?"

"Yes, Bernd. Claude and the others were there, too, and we are now working together on the new plans. Claude should be able to describe the worst-case scenario after talking to the professor's team about the details. "

"I hope Claude will come to the conference soon. He seems very distracted lately, missing deadlines and not reported in like he usually does. Anne, how are things with the government and with the local builders? And when do we have the green light for the test buildings?"

Before she could answer, Claude interrupted. "Sorry for the delay, folks! I must have overheard the alarm clock. I'm sorry. Bernd, please give me a signal when I should report the latest news on the state of the blueprints. "

"Claude, is everything all right with you? This is not the first time you've been late lately. Please wait until Anne is finished, then you can report on the situation."

The new MOOC plans are waiting. Bernd indirectly blames Claude for this, and he calls for accountability. Later, he regrets speaking so harshly to Claude.

When Claude's turn came, he could not say how the MOOC plans would go. There was now only one team of professors working on the blueprints and they took Pilar's suggestions as a basis. But they could not name an appointment until they were ready. The professors were working parallel on different courses and projects, and they needed an additional workshop before they feel that they could make accurate predictions.

"Claude, you know me, and you know I can't rest until we have a clear deadline," Bernd said. "Should I talk to the professors in New York and encourage them to move faster?"

"Bernd, pressure is the last thing we need right now. We'll be doing the workshop this week, and then I'll tell you about the results."

"That's not enough, Claude. I want to have a status report every two days until the final date for the project is final.

Stella hooked in: "Claude, would you make sure that the current project plan is on the drive so that Anne, Pilar, and the others can watch the latest version?"

"Will do, Stella."

"People, thank you once again for your commitment. Claude, we need to talk tomorrow evening."

Bernd ended the conference with an uneasy feeling for his comments to Claude. The Canadian was a key figure in this project. Perhaps Bernd should not have criticized him so openly?

Just as he thought this, Linda called him over Skype.

"Hello Linda, nice to hear from you again. You do not call often, what's going on? "

Linda finds that Bernd was too harsh on Claude. She explains what is going on in Claude's life, and Bernd is worried because he didn't know how his friend Claude was doing.

"Bernd, I think you were a little hard on Claude. Do you know about Maria? Claude is in love. He skypes with her for hours on end and flies to Rome on weekends to see her. You might want some patience with him. You know that love gives us wings, but it also makes us blind..."

"Oh, I didn't know. Thank you for telling me. I thought Claude and I were friends. Why didn't he tell me? How do you know about it? "

"We've been on a lot of telephone conferences together in the past months, and we always start with a personal exchange. That is how we know what is going on with the others and how we can better deal with each other."

Bernd answered somewhat surprised, "Okay, if this helps you to cooperate better with each other, then it's all right."

"Would you consider doing this for our joint conferences with the whole team as well?"

"Look, this seems unfamiliar to me, and I'm not sure if it makes any sense. But I'll ask Paul for advice. I wanted to report to him anyway."

"Thank you, Bernd." Linda hung up.

Paul had offered Bernd that he could call spontaneously whenever he needed help. Until now Bernd had not made use of the offer. Bernd was delighted at how well he and his team were doing and how independently and self-reliably everyone was working. The workshop had paid off.

Bernd wondered what he could do to improve the performance of the team. Could Linda be right? Was he giving too little room for sharing personal experiences? He decided to call Paul.

"Hello Bernd, how are you?" Paul asked on the phone with his quiet voice.

Bernd calls his mentor, Paul, and gets feedback on team communication. Paul says there needs to be more exchange with each other about personal matters. Bernd should build a relationship with everyone on the team.

"I'm fine, Paul. I hope with you as well. Before we talk about other things, I have to tell you that the results of the workshop have far exceeded my expectations. Everyone on my team is taking the initiative to get the job done, to bring others on board when they need it, and to find solutions. They are really doing great! We have not yet achieved an important milestone, but I think that is more of a communication problem than bad project management or lack of skills."

"Very good, Bernd. Your people are working together as a real team and you seem to be enjoying it. I have a question: how often are your team meetings and what is your agenda?"

"Well, we talk once a month. In the event that problems occur, we schedule an additional meeting. As for the agenda, I usually prepare and send it in advance."

"Okay. And what about the participation in your discussions?"

"Well, there are the usual suspects. Claude usually dominates the conversation. The others join in if what we are talking about is of interest to them or from their area. Linda is something like our feeling and inter-relational barometer. She always senses when someone is not doing well or if something has gone wrong. If someone does not deliver for personal reasons, then she knows the reason. She seems to have built a relationship with everyone on the team."

"And you?" Paul asked. "Have you built a relationship with everyone on the team?"

"Let me put it this way: I get along with everyone. I make sure that we can concentrate on the important things when we have our monthly calls. And I make sure that everyone delivers results. That's how I see my role. During our last conference call, I had a little run-in with Claude. He was somewhat passive, and he almost missed a deadline. He even accidentally woke me up in the middle of the night. Linda seems to think that he is in love."

"Are you not friends with Claude? I thought you told me that when we met."

"Yes, I am, actually. Perhaps, I don't show enough interest in people. Linda is of the opinion that we should allow time during our monthly calls to exchange information about our personal lives. What do you think?"

"In virtual teams," Paul continued, "it is especially important that the team members regularly talk about how they are doing personally. In my experience, it works really well to allow time during the weekly telephone conference to find out how everyone is doing in their private lives. It's best to give everyone a certain timeslot to share".

"Every week?" Bernd sounded surprised and a little unenthusiastic. "Is that not too often? And is it not boring when everyone bares their soul in front everyone else?"

"You'd be surprised. People are not boring, nor will they be bored at learning how the others are doing. Our personal lives have a huge impact on our professional lives," Paul explained. "It is important to be able to recognize the mood of the group. I'm not saying that each person should tell and endless story about their lives. Give each team member two minutes to talk about how they are doing in their private lives. Two minutes should be more than enough. But make sure that every single person gets the two minutes. Otherwise, the more introverted team members will not say anything, and you won't have any idea of how they are doing.

Following Paul's advice, Bernd wants to propose a new communication structure for the project. There should be a weekly, rather informal conference where both personal and project-oriented things will be discussed and a monthly more formal, even with the external partners.

"These two minutes make the difference between you knowing how your people are doing, and you not knowing anything about them. And not just you. The other team members need to know how their colleagues are doing, and they need to have the others know how they are doing."

Paul continued, "When you are just having update conference calls, you can just concentrate on the important topics at hand. Afterwards, people can contact each other by e-mail or get together in smaller groups to solve any problems that may come up."

"That sounds okay so far," Bernd answered, "but I am concerned that we will lose focus on the big picture and on our ultimate goals if we speak too long on personal issues and small details about the project."

That danger does exist," Paul said. "That is why I hold conferences once a month which have a different structure. These meetings are much more formal, and we do not discuss anything personal. Every person has to submit a one-page report on how far they believe they are in reaching the yearly goals we established at the workshop. I also invite the most important partners from outside the team to these conference calls, so that everyone – the core team and our partners – is informed of how things are going. If there is something confidential that needs to be discussed, we save these points for the end of the conference after the others have left the conference room. In this way, you have a weekly less formal meeting in which project details, personal issues, and the greatest challenges are discussed, and once a month you have a more formal strategic planning session to discuss the implementation of details and to make sure that no one loses sight of the big picture."

"That sounds sensible. I'm a little concerned that everything will become a bit bureaucratic."

"I highly recommend it, Bernd." Paul answered. "With this structure, you will have a better overview of everything – both where the project is and how your people are doing. And that's without an additional time commitment on your side. And do you know what yet another advantage is?" asked Paul.

"What?" asked Bernd.

"You will never again miss out on finding out if someone on your team is in love!"

"Alright," Bernd said, smiling. "It's not my usual style, but, if you say so, I'll give it a try!"

Set Up a Communication Structure as Early as Possible

Every time I am assigned to run a virtual team, I call together the core team in the first week. These are the people with whom I will be directly working, and to begin we start with a live, in-person workshop. In the first chapter, you read about how such a workshop usually goes. In this chapter, we will concentrate on to best set up the communication channels for after the workshop, so that your team keeps its momentum.

At the end of the workshop, I ask my team how often we should speak with other? By this I mean, how often should a team conference call take place. Most of the time, people say that once a month is enough. I try to provoke them by saying, "Let's try talking once every week. If you find this to be too often, we can always change it."

At the beginning of the project, roughly 60% to 70% of the team show up at these weekly conference calls. After about one month, roughly 90% to 100% of the team start showing up, and this quota stays until the end of the project. What is the secret behind these intensive meetings? It's the personal contact.

Normally, I start every weekly team conference with a general update. During the week, I receive many e-mails. I immediately direct those who require immediate action to the person who is responsible for the respective areas. But I

In the weekly conferences, not only the progress of work should be discussed, but also personal matters. This strengthens bonding and increases participation and motivation.

deliberately save the e-mails which serve to inform me about progress on the project for these weekly meetings. As manager, you will have to take part in different meetings at many different levels. Make sure that you allow time in the weekly conference call to summarize the results of your conversations with other decision makers. Discuss with your team what was decided on in these other meetings. If you don't take these few minutes to keep your team informed, you will find that rumors may start to be spread. This may lead to mistrust or other unnecessary problems.

This general update ultimately revolves around all relevant events during the past week. It gives the team members the opportunity to ask questions and get rid of false observations or rumors. After this round, everyone in the team has a fixed timeslot to report what is happening to him both personally and with regard to the project. Thanks to the first workshop, they know each other's personal and professional lifelines. During the weekly conferences, we always come back to the personal level. This creates real interpersonal relationships. A fixed timeslot is particularly important for the more quiet and introverted team members, who prefer to be silent and listen instead of sharing, if they are not assigned their own speaking time.

The more formal monthly conference is predominantly for the core team members and usually takes place through a video conference. With these meetings, it is important that each core team member reports on his or her progress on the project and how their team is. I believe it is very important and it builds trust to see your colleagues at least once per month. These monthly conferences also give us the opportunity to invite others from outside the core team to the meeting, so that they may learn first-hand how the project is progressing. If they have questions or need additional information, this meeting is an ideal place to ask. The questions that are asked are gathered in the chat column of the conference call. We then allow ten minutes at the end of the meeting to answer these questions.

In the case of a more formalized monthly conference, it is important to provide a larger body with first-hand information and to allow them to ask questions.

If there are important decisions that have to be addressed, for example, if someone wishes to give change directions and work on another part of the project, these decisions should be made during the monthly conference. This is the best platform to lay out all relevant information for and with all of the important decision makers. Afterwards all of the core team members and the extended participants should pass the results of this meeting on to their own teams, if they have employees with whom they are working. This should be done, not in a top-down fashion, but in an interactive way during a meeting or telephone conference. Everyone who has something to do with the project should have the chance to ask questions or to give feedback.

Method:
Make sure that your weekly telephone conferences have a healthy mix between personal and project-oriented updates as well as formal and informal reports on each team member's progress.

Another advantage of holding formal monthly conferences is a healthy level of pressure. Every team member has to report on their goals and ambitions. If someone is behind schedule or does not reach their goals at all, it becomes visible to the entire team. If goals are interlinked, as they should be, the goals of one team member always depend on the goals of at least one other team member. If someone has problems, then offer support. The responsibility, however, should remain with the team member, him- or herself. Of course, there can also be conflicts, and not every conflict can be resolved during a conference call. Nevertheless, a certain pressure is important to increase the performance of the entire team.

The Art of Divvying Time at Team Meetings

Both for the weekly conferences as well as for the monthly conferences, it is crucial to have a good, clear time management. There should be a clear-cut agenda with realistic time allocations built in, so that each person knows how much time they have to speak on a particular subject. It is also recommended to name someone at the beginning of each conference to the timekeeper. The timekeeper monitors the time and has permission to interrupt the others if they go too long. The timekeeper should not be the team leader or the leader of the conference. The team leader should be free to give feedback and praise team members for what they have accomplished. The team leader also needs to be free to resolve conflicts and shouldn't generally squander his authority by having to constantly refer to the time schedule.

Up to ten or twelve team members participate in a weekly conference. Since there is always a general update at the beginning of the conference and then every team member has two minutes to share personal and project-related topics, you should schedule an hour and a half for the full confer-

A scheduled, precise agenda is as important as ending the meeting punctually. It is best to appoint a timekeeper who will make sure that everyone stays in their timeslot.

ence. Conferences longer than one-and-a-half hours are ineffective. You would then need to allow for breaks, and during breaks, people check their e-mails or phone messages and are simply no longer focused on the conference call.

To finish your conference call on time is important if you want to keep participation at 90% to 100%. In absolute exceptional cases, you may ask all of the participants if they would be willing to go ten more minutes to discuss an important topic. After those 10 minutes, however, you need to stop the meeting!

At a monthly conference, up to 100 people can meet for large projects. I recommend two hours for this. In virtual teams, punctuality and time allotments are even more important than in local teams. If the team members are also distributed to different time zones, bad time management is even more detrimental.

Method:

Experience has shown that you should allow the following criteria for your weekly and monthly conferences:

* **Weekly Conference** – more personal and project-related information and updates

  Length of Conference: 1.5 Hours

- **Monthly Conference** – more formal updates and participation from the extended teams

  Length of Conference: 2 Hours

Time management and ending the meeting punctually are extremely important in both cases!

What Time of Day Should Conferences Take Place?

Based on my experience, a typical global telephone conference should start in Europe at noon. Then it is already evening in Australia and other parts of Asia. If the team member is already at home, then you may hear dogs barking in the background, children screaming or eating dishes. At this same time, it is early morning in North and South America. Here the team member may have just woken up and is still in his bathrobe. To recognize these differences and to openly speak about them brings the team together and helps it bond. Your team members will also appreciate it if the calling times change on occasion, so that they are not always stuck with an unpleasant time. No one, however, should have to participate too late in the evening or too early in the morning.

If you have very important news for the team members around the world, it is an option to make two identical conference calls the same day: one in the morning for Europe, Australia, Asia and Africa and one in the afternoon for North and South America. Europeans can choose whether they prefer to participate in the morning or in the afternoon session.

If they hold worldwide conferences in English, they will have to do with many people who are not native speakers and who may speak with an accent. Even native speakers speak very differently depending on where they come from, for example, England, Scotland, Texas or Australia. One complaint that often comes up is that someone else cannot speak English well. The Indian, for example, does not understand the French, while the Indians understand one another very well.

For conferences in English, the team leader should make sure that everyone can be understood. Native speakers should be asked to speak more slowly and clearly. Participants with a strong accent should write parallel in the chat.

As a team leader, you can do a lot to improve the intelligibility. For example, ask the native speaker to speak slowly and not to use too difficult expressions. In general, using simple language helps everyone to understand. If someone has proven to have a particularly difficult accent, you can ask them to submit their questions or comments in advance or to use the chat box when communicating. This creates clarity and helps to create a more relaxed atmosphere. It is important that everyone thinks not only about themselves, but also about the others and that each person does his or her best to be understood.

Simplification of communication is important. If possible, schedule team meetings on the same day of the week at the same time and over the same communication channel. The exception to this rule is with global conferences. There, as mentioned above, you should try to vary the meeting time or create two identical meetings, so that not just one party is constantly being inconvenienced.

Explore Different Points of View in Your Team

Normally in virtual teams, a lot of e-mails get sent back and forth. In most cases, something is either being asked for in the e-mail or some information is being sent. E-mail, however, is not a particularly interactive medium.

Team conferences, on the other hand, are synchronous communication tools and are therefore the ideal place to hold a discussion. A discussion means not only asking for or giving others something, but also understanding each other. Free, open discussions should be encouraged during your conference calls. Conference calls give you an ideal platform to discuss conflict situations or new challenges that have arisen. In a conference call the team is able to find solutions together.

In his book *The Fifth Discipline,* Peter M. Senge distinguishes between "Advocacy" and "Inquiry." In management, the typical behavior is to take a stand on an issue and advocate for it. The goal is to defend our opinions and influence others. We are not interested in inquiring about or understanding other standpoint or opinions. Senge argues that it is far better to begin by trying to understand the opinions of others before we establish and announce our own opinions. In a team culture, where there are many different ideas and opinions and conflicts can occur, it is important to find a balance between advocacy and inquiry. Each person on the team has a right to his own opinions, but he should try to understand the opinions of others. The team leader has to set an example here by asking questions and trying himself to understand the different opinions of different team members. He should encourage lively, constructive conversations and should be careful not to override the others with his own opinions.

An "inquisitive" attitude is the key to good team communication, especially in conflict situations. First understand others, then advocate for your standpoint.

In my seminars, participants often complain that their team leader only calls a meeting together if there are problems. Many than waste time by using the meeting to defend themselves, to blame others for problems, or to announce that they have come up with the solution. In some cultures, this authoritarian way for leaders to act is expected. In these cultures, it is expected that the boss has all of the answers when problems arise.

In virtual teams, however, this type of behavior creates many more problems than it solves. There is already a very limited amount of time available on a conference call, and when this precious time is filled with blaming others or dictating solutions, it is very counterproductive. Virtual teams have greater need to discuss about a situation with each other than in face-to-face meetings. That is why virtual teams need communication structures which allow each person to express his or her opinions. When conflicts arise or controversial discussions take place, the team leader needs to make sure that the team finds the balance between advocacy and inquiry.

How to Give Regular, Constructive, Individual Feedback

Structured communication in virtual teams is essentially three-fold: first, regular team meetings, with the right balance of personal and project-related information, alternating both in the informal and the formal framework. Second, the opportunity for genuine dialogue and exchange, beyond merely advocating for your own opinion. And third, regular one-to-one feedback with your team members on both project performance and personal development, such as team skills or soft skills. Not only team meetings, but also feedback to individual team members, should take place regularly and be very structured. Under no circumstances should the team leader give feedback only when problems arise.

Team members need regular one-to-one feedbacks on both performance and personal development. A monthly call is perfect for this.

In my virtual teams, I called every team member who reported directly to me once a month. It was important to me to discuss their progress and whether or not they were reaching their objectives. If it were necessary to give critical feedback, I always did this in the one-to-one meetings. I recommend never giving critical feedback by e-mail and certainly not during a conference in front of other team members. The one-to-one discussions, however, are not just to give criticism. The conversations are a special opportunity for each team member to get in touch with the leader. The team leader gives feedback, but this is not a one-way street. The team member should take the opportunity to seek advice and support where necessary.

Typically, the individual feedback conversations should be divided in half: 50% is about the team member progress and 50% is for feedback and support from the team leader. It is important to ask: How can I support you? Or, can I do anything to make your work even better? During these monthly one-to-one conversations, the team leader and the team member decide themselves how they benefit from the meeting. Such one-on-one conversations are also a great platform to show appreciation for the individual team member. Therefore, they should never be canceled at short notice, without immediately offering alternative dates.

I think it is good to do a formal performance assessment roughly twice a year. This can also be done during the individual feedback calls, although it is even better to do this personally in a face-to-face meeting. In this type of formal assessment, it is important to have objectively measurable achievements by means of clear indicators. These conversations should be based on a comprehensible process which gives the executive the opportunity to intervene if necessary. In addition to the performance assessment, I recommend talking about the developmental goals of the respective team member. What other competences or leadership skills would the team member want to develop in the near future? There should be a concrete plan for this

Group feedback should take place twice a year, be well prepared, and have a clear structure. Criticism can only relate to the behavior of a person present and not to the person himself.

assessment, and depending on the results, the company should ensure mentoring or training to help the team member reach his goals.

All these monthly and semi-annual individual feedback meetings are without question time-consuming, but it is an investment of the team leader in his team. The team pays back these investments manifold by being more proactive and forward-looking. Good communication is the key to greater commitment and success -- even over great distances.

Group Feedback - Opportunity in the Personal Meetings

Another form of feedback in virtual teams is the group feedback. I recommend it once or twice a year, especially if there is an opportunity is for a face-to-face meeting. For the group feedback the team members are best placed seated in a circle. Starting with team leader, each team member receives feedback on the following three points:

1. **What to do next?** What has been done well and where did someone support the team particularly well? It is often refreshing and motivating to be told that you have accomplished a lot. Especially in virtual teams, many team members don't see their contributions to the whole hand what has become of them. These meetings give the team leader the chance to share these successes and to thank the team members in front of everyone.

2. **What to stop doing?** Where is there need for improvement? Here, for example, we are talking about so-called "blind spots." Blind spots are something that a person is unaware of which may be causing harm to others, annoying others, or stopping others from reaching their goals. When discussing blind spots, it is important to use nonviolent and empathetic verbage. Do not let it become personal. It is always about the behavior, never about the person!

3. **What to start with?** What potential does someone have? This feedback is about identifying skills that a team member has, but is still not using enough. The group invites the team member to develop these skills and to use them more often.

The preparation for the feedback round is very important. Each team member should answer the above questions for every other team member in advance. When they write it down, it ensures that not only do they have something to share during the meeting, but they also will tend to stick by their opinions when sharing with the other, instead of being influenced by the opinions of others.

At the end of the feedback round, each participant writes a written summary of the advice he or she was given: What to do next? What to stop doing? And what to start with? They then send this document to the team leader, so that they have it for the next individual feedback meeting.

> *A team charter gives the team some guidelines for its work together. It should always be created by the entire team. The more cultures involved, the more important it is.*

The Benefits of a Team Charter

You now have a set of principles for structured communication in your virtual team.

Each team, however, is unique in terms of its composition, its objectives and its social and economic environment. In order to take into account these factors, individual agreements for an optimal communication culture can be made. To this end, many teams are now developing a so-called team charter. This determines how members of the team have agreed to deal with each other. A team charter should always be developed jointly, preferably through a live, face-to-face workshop.

The following questions can help your team to make meaningful arrangements for regular communication in its team charter:

* What types of team meetings do we want to have?

* On which technical platform and at what times do our conferences take place?

* How often do we speak and who takes part?

* What is the agenda and what is the timeframe?

* Which one-on-one discussions are there with the team leader and when do they take place?

* What communication channels do we use with the team? (i.e., e-mail, telephone, voice-mail, text message and video conferencing)

* How much response time is allowed to answer an e-mail?

* Which communication channel do we use in urgent situations? (i.e., Voice-mail on the mobile phone or WhatsApp)

- What is the maximum response time that should be allowed on the communication channel for urgent cases?

The bigger the team is and the more cultures and different time zones are affected, the more important it is to have a team charter. We all have our personal communication style. One person likes to telephone, the other prefers to write e-mails. A third is particularly active on social media and loves WhatsApp. And so on. So that the team does not go according to the preferences of individuals, it is important that everyone agrees. In addition, there are cultural peculiarities. In Germany, for example, it is not usual to call a team member in the evening or on the weekend, unless you have explicitly agreed to. In Mexico, leaving a voice-mail on the mobile phone is an everyday communication channel. In Europe, this is only done in urgent situations. All of these different habits and cultural impressions need to be discussed in your virtual team and agreed upon. This creates standards and norms that greatly facilitate collaboration and healthy communication within your virtual team.

Chapter 8

Structure and Processes Create the Basis – Trust Unlocks the Team's Power

Bernd looked at the current status report. They have been in the construction phase for three months. The foundations and very unique, resistant structures were already in place. He was delighted as he watched the project continue to grow without him having to do much intervention.

Claude was back on track and ensured smooth communication among the various parties. Anne was responsible for the construction progress, supported by Pilar and Linda. Stella was strictly aware of the rules of document management. An extended leadership team had formed on Linda's initiative. This included all the key personnel who reported directly to the core team, for example the managers of local construction companies and engineering firms.

After the professors and students voted for the three best student contributions to the architectural contest, the professor in New York honored the winners, and they, too, were asked to be on the extended management team. They participated in the monthly video conference, asked questions via chat, and introduced their ideas.

"Wow," thought Bernd, "we are quite a lot now, and the ideas are just flowing!"

In fact, the extended team had once again given some ideas for refining the blueprints. An Asian professor, who had already been involved in the original MOOC, had set up another team that was now documenting best practices.

What was Bernd doing? He also had his own ideas for improvement and gave the team regular feedback. During the rest of his time, he devoted himself to important stakeholders, such as government representatives in Transmontania. Twice he had already flown to the capital to discuss the project and to strengthen his relationship to some of the key players. Earlier this would have been unthinkable because of a lack of time. Tomorrow he had a telephone conference with the manager of one of the most important construction companies on site, a Chinese company. Anne and the Minister for Development of Transmontania would be there. The chances for further contracts in Asia were good.

Bernd is satisfied. Everything is going steadily. Claude is back on track. Linda has created an extended team. Bernd dreams of major orders in Asia.

Bernd looked out of the window at harbor, the Elbe and the horizon. In his head, he saw the skyline of an Asian metropolis full of buildings built by his company with even larger virtual teams. Bernd was almost a little euphoric. Not only because of the business opportunities, but also because of the prospect of many new and interesting people that he could get to know and inspire. He would get to know most of them only virtually, but he would still be able to build strong relationships and collaborate very personally with them. Bernd decided to end this day sooner, just to celebrate how much he had achieved. He asked his assistant to reserve a table for two people in his wife's favorite restaurant. Wiebke was enthusiastic when she heard about it by SMS. It had been several months since they last had a romantic evening out.

Bernd had already found a parking place near the restaurant, when he decided to check his emails one last time. Immediately, he saw an email from Anne in the inbox of the iPhone, whose subject line began with uppercase letters. It read:

URGENT: Construction work will take longer.

Bernd held his breath and clutched his phone tightly, as if he wanted to squeeze the bad news out of it. "Stay calm," Bernd said out loud, as if hearing his own voice made it easier. He frantically read through the email and then read it again more carefully.

It had been proven that Pilar's new ideas reduced material costs, but now everything is taking longer. Because of this, we have two problems: First, the date of actually handing the keys over to their new owner will be threateningly close to the start of winter. Second, the additional work involved will cost additional money -- money which was to be saved by the altered blueprints and new building materials. The budget was supposed to be set. Non-negotiable. Now what do we do?

Bernd's high spirits were blown away. He was no longer in the mood to celebrate. On the contrary. "Constant changes, winter is closing in, and a super-tight budget - why do I actually do this?" Bernd asked himself. "In Germany, it is so much easier to plan and build something." Bernd hit the steering wheel with his fist.

But half a minute later, he asked himself, "Who can help us this time?" He had to think about all the problems he had already solved with his virtual team. He thought about the workshop with Paul, the very successful Crowdfunding, and the new design. Will we make it again this time? And what will I tell the minister tomorrow?

Suddenly, Bernd had an idea: "What if I just give the team a hard deadline? I can tell them that it has to be done by this deadline, no if's, and's, or but's. I can also tell them that it may not exceed our budgetary requirements. Then

Just as Bernd was about to celebrate his success, he is informed a critical delay in the construction work. He decides to trust his team.

they will to think about it and find a solution." In Germany, Bernd had never done this before. His timetables had always been realistic and all his budgets had been met. This, however, was a completely different situation now.

And the minister? "Well, I will just have to tell him the truth! I will have to tell him that we still do not know if we will be ready on time, because we are breaking new ground. None of this has ever been tried before. I will tell him that I trust my team 100%."

At that moment, he saw the faces of Claude, Anne, Linda, Pilar and Stella. He also saw the faces of the young people from the MOOC, which he only knew from video conferences. This afternoon he could only think about new houses and an impressive skyline. Now he can only think about his people. His instinct told him, "Yes, I trust them. It's true. I fully trust them."

"Okay, I'm going to do it," Bernd said loudly to himself. He got out of his BMW and locked it. "Even if it means putting my reputation on the line!"

When Bernd entered the restaurant, he saw Wiebke already sitting at the table he had reserved in front of the panoramic window. The view of the evening harbor was spectacular. Wiebke turned to him as he got closer and smiled at him.

The next morning, Bernd put on an elegant dark suit and tied his tie. The video conference with the minister and the Chinese manager was the most important event on his schedule today. It was very strange to be the only person who was not physically in Transmania. The others would be in the minister's office.

At 11:00 a.m., Bernd sat in his office, drank a sip of water, cleared his throat and then started WebEx. The conference began in a very formal and cool tone.

In a video conference with the minister and a Chinese manager, Bernd promises that the work will take a maximum of four weeks longer. He still has no solution to the problem.

In a very reserved manner, the Transmontanian minister praised the good progress with which the project was forward, in particular the fact that they were using local workers and materials. He then made it clear that he could not tolerate any delays in the schedule. His credibility and the popularity of his party were at stake. They had made a promise to the people, and he wanted to keep this promise. Then he asked, "When exactly will the buildings be finished?"

Bernd made his decision. One month later than planned, his team would be ready with everything.

Anne then made a suggestion: "As a Plan B, why not first complete the schools and use them as a shelter for the families whose houses would not be ready by winter?" They agreed to make a decision about Plan B within the next two weeks.

When the conference was over, Bernd loosened his tie and leaned back on his swivel chair. He even put his feet upon on his desk, something he very rarely did. It's happened! He has given his word and risked his good reputation without having a fool-proof plan. There was only trust. There were no guarantees.

Later that afternoon, Bernd called Paul to discuss the current development.

"How are you, Bernd?" Paul asked in a good mood. "I've read your latest status report. Seems you're doing really well."

"Paul, I thought, too, that until yesterday evening. Then, out of the blue, it suddenly became clear that we needed more time and money.

With the new construction plans, we have lower material costs, but we have to spend more time. This has increased our labor costs. And do you know what I did today? I promised the minister that we would need a maximum of one month longer. My God! I don't know how we are going do it -- let alone where we are going to get the extra money! You probably think I'm crazy now. But I had a good feeling, despite the risk."

"I do not think you're crazy at all," Paul said. "You just have confidence in your team, and you are firmly convinced that you will find a solution together."

"Well, at the moment we have not even integrated the new extended team into our meetings. But somehow, I am confident that if they put their heads together, they will find a solution. "

"Bernd, I know a tool and a process that will help you with this. Would you like to try it?"

"There are many coaching tools," Bernd answered without thinking what he was saying.

"Bernd, I see that the team is making real progress," continued Paul. "My next suggestion would have been to do a feedback round anyway, with all of them giving feedback on three points: What should we continue doing? What should we stop doing? and, where should we begin? In this round, you can also use this tool and solve the new problem."

Paul advises Bernd to believe in his team and to trust that they will find a solution. He also proposes a special workshop for problem solving.

"Should I invite the extended team?" Bernd asked.

"Not for the feedback round. All you need is your core team. In order for a feedback round to work, the participants have to have established a relationship with each other and have already experienced a lot together. Your core team has this relationship.

"Later, for the problem-solving session, we should bring in the extended team. Everyone will profit from having further experience in the room."

"Okay, Paul. You convinced me once again."

The combined workshop for group feedback and problem solving was scheduled on a short notice for the following Monday. Luckily, Linda was in London anyway and could fly over to Hamburg to personally be there. Claude moved the next romantic weekend with Maria, his new friend from Barcelona, to Hamburg. He could just stay in the city on Monday to attend the workshop. Anne and the managers from the construction companies should stay in Asia and participate by video-conference. The professor and a young Asian colleague would join in from New York. Pilar, Stella and Paul would stay at home and log in to WebEx via their computers. The budget was tight. Therefore, the team did everything to keep the travel costs low.

The workshop takes place in Hamburg and by videocon-ference at five other locations. Bernd explains the situation, and everyone are ready to go the extra mile.

When the day of the work-shop came, Bernd, Claude and Linda gathered in Hamburg in Bernd's conference room. It was a sunny day, and through the large windows one could see how the sunlight made the Elbe sparkle. The interesting light play repeated itself on the ceiling of the room.

All three were sitting at the conference table, their laptops were opened, and they were ready for the video conference. Bernd went through the agenda once more, while Claude and Linda had already begun a robust discussion.

At 1 p.m., Bernd started the conference.

"Hello and good day in the round! I am glad that everyone is on time. We are now in six places: in Hamburg, Rio, Transmontania, in Sofia, in Georgetown on the Cayman Islands, and in New York City. There are twelve of us here. This is truly a global conference! As we all know, we are making great strides in the construction of earthquake-proof houses. However, the adjustment of the blueprints has led to some delays. On the one hand, we have to speed up the construction process and, on the other hand, save money on the unavoidable additional working." Bernd took a deep breath.

"In this situation, I have done something that I have never dared to do before in my entire career as an entrepreneur. On behalf of the entire team, I have announced a completion date without having a detailed plan. In concrete terms, this means we have one additional month to get everything ready. This has already been decided. The government will pay the construction workers their salaries one month longer. We have to pay for all other additional costs.

"This means that we need a whole new approach. We need a break-through! We need to find a way to catch up on the delay and save money at the same time. We've got to win this fight. It is the fight against the onset of winter. When winter comes, all the families need to have a roof over their heads. We have already set priorities again and are finishing the schools first. There, we can accommodate the families whose houses are not yet finished before the cold sets in. By then they have to be out of the tents. I am convinced that as a team we will win this fight. I put my good reputation on the line by making this promise, because I know we will find a solution together. Can I rely on you all? Are you ready to fight against the winter and all technical hurdles?"

Bernd heard some say, "Yes." He saw others agree by nodding, both in the room and on the video screen. He knew that their "Yes" was not just a "Yes." Their "Yes" means: "Yes, we are willing and ready to go the extra mile, so the project becomes a success. We stand behind this 100%!"

Bernd felt the feeling of ease and gratitude come back. They had reached a new level of trust and commitment in the team. And that felt really good.

Now it was Paul's turn. He explained his special method of brainstorming.

"For our meeting today, each of you has completed the Visual Questionnaire. On the basis of your profiles I divided you into four groups. I call these the virtual brainstorming groups, and I have already set them up on our new online tool.

Paul directs the brainstorming to find a solution to the problem. The team works in four groups formed according to their personality profiles. In the end, they have groundbreaking ideas and new scenarios.

"Please look at the group to which you belong. Each of you in your group should brainstorm on the following question: How can we speed up the construction process while staying on the original budget? You have 45 minutes to discuss it and to come up with a solution. Afterwards, each group will present their results. Do you have any questions?"

You could tell that the team was getting excited. The regular conferences of the extended leadership team now paid off. All of them had the essential construction principles in mind and knew the status of the current construction progress.

Bernd, Stella and the professor were part of the strategic group. They were visionaries, saw the big picture, thought in different scenarios and were passionate about the subject. Bernd saw the other two on his laptop. Despite the distance, there was a lively discussion. The group wrote their ideas on a virtual whiteboard. Bernd has no become very good at giving others space in their creativity and taking every idea seriously. Even if he disagreed completely, he did not immediately object, but asked questions to understand the intention behind every proposal.

After 45 minutes the group had an action plan. They knew what additional research would be necessary. They could even quantify the efficiency gain. It was time for the presentation.

The creative group, consisting of Claude, Pilar and Edwin, the junior professor from Asia, suggested to test whether certain components can be produced in a 3-D printer. This would save time and money. A group of students, led by Professor Tan, has already done research in this area. The students had discovered this new trend themselves. In China, they were already having great successes with the 3-D printing of similar parts, which remained largely unknown in the West.

For Bernd, it was the light at the end of the tunnel. The best thing was that all four groups presented their results from different perspectives. There was a groundbreaking new idea for the use of materials, there were new scenarios for risk management, and there was a communication strategy to gain the full support of the population, government and non-governmental organizations.

Bernd fell a stone lifted from the heart. His team was fantastic! People had once again surpassed his expectations. Still deeply moved, Bernd finished the conference in words he'd never used before: "I'm proud to lead this team. And I am firmly convinced that this team will surpass itself. We'll write history."

Processes are Good, Trust is Better

What do a virtual team and the universe have in common? Well, the universe consists of only 10% matter. These are the planets and stars. 20 percent is nothing - black holes and other phenomena which cannot yet be explained by science. And 70 percent of the universe is invisible energy. This includes, for example, the gravitational force. It holds the universe together. A virtual team is quite similar. Only 10% of the team is its members and the infrastructure. This is, so to speak, the matter. 20% are undeveloped potentials.

And 70% are the relationships, the trust, that is, the gravitational force that holds the virtual team together. The art of running a virtual team is to focus on this 70%. Make sure that the gravitational force is strong. You will be amazed at how much you can improve your results by focusing entirely on relationships and trust.

Trust is the main factor that holds virtual teams together. Anyone who wants better results should focus on this.

Now, you may disagree: A team needs efficient structures, processes, rules and procedures. This is not wrong. There are various methods for process optimization. For example, Lean Management, Agile Management, Scrum or Kanban are such methods. But more importantly are the interpersonal relationships on the team, the ability to work independently, and self-discipline. With all of these there is a common denominator: Trust.

Structures and processes are unquestionably important. The more virtual the team, the more the interaction between the team members has to be institutionalized. A process, an agenda or a certain role distribution ensures efficiency.

In Chapter 7, I presented you with various forms of regular team interaction, which provide both a clear structure and content flexibility. This includes the informal weekly conference with its personal and project-related updates, as well as the formal monthly conference, which focuses on the state of the progress of the team in working toward its goal.

At the monthly conferences, the extended management team is present, which consists of everyone who reports directly to the core team. This ensures that strategic guidelines penetrate all hierarchical levels and that everyone is informed of the progress of the project. In Bernd's team, this was a prerequisite for a breakthrough, when a solution was urgently needed for faster construction progress.

Without the use of regular, trusted processes, virtual teams cannot function. The deciding factors, however, are interpersonal relationships and self-discipline. Moreover, it is more important to have clear objectives and to promote individual respon-

The more virtual a team, the higher the need for commitment. Processes are important; however, flexibility and individual responsibility are even more vital.

sibility rather than to hold on to pre-defined processes. Processes can become tedious. What I mean by this is that they build on the results of the previous step and take into account the feedback from customers and other stakeholders for the next step.

In virtual power teams, it is essential that everyone has a clear annual goal and that they can decide for themselves how best to achieve it. At the same time, there must be processes which ensure a constant exchange with the most important stakeholders. The customer perspective is enormously important and should be constantly considered before going on to the next development stage. Scrum defines roles, for example the "product owner." The "product owner" acts as if he were the client's lawyer. He takes the perspective of his client and explains his needs to the team. The "Scrum Master", in turn, organizes the communication and ensures compliance with agreed rules in the individual phases of the project.

The Process Master should be the Primary Coordinator of the Team

In order for processes to run smoothly, there should be a "process master" or coordinator who ensures that everyone adheres to the agreed rules. This person can, at the same time, be responsible for the agenda and the observance of the time frame during meetings. In my teams, I have often assigned this role to the person who was also responsible for the document management and the electronic directories.

The person responsible for document management in virtual teams is often also well suited to be the team coordinator.

The coordinator then defines the conventions, such as the naming of documents or the filing, to which the team agrees and ensures that everyone respects them. The coordinator is also responsible for the smooth functioning of the conferences, and they ensure that each person has time to express his or her thoughts on issues. In Bernd's team Stella took over the role of the coordinator. She has very good IT knowledge and has enough authority to enforce the agreed upon rules.

Giving team members specific roles is even more important in virtual teams than in local teams. It creates clarity and ensures smooth processes. These roles, however, must not distract from the fact that everyone should be goal-oriented and individually responsible for achieving these goals.

Individual responsibility on the basis of trust is always more important than to be a slave to certain processes.

Helpful regular questions for a week conference:

- How did I help our team achieve its goals last week?

- What do I want to do this week to help the team achieve their goals even better?

- What hurdles do I see that make it harder for me or the team to achieve the goals?

A wonderful story which illustrates what I mean is the victory of Admiral Nelson against the Spanish armada. At the beginning of the 19th century, naval battles were always the same. The ships floated parallel to each other and shot at the other side with cannons. The "process" of how a naval battle was to be conducted was precisely defined, and there were whole libraries which described it.

The formation of the fleet and the command chains were, as well, defined as the question of when to shoot and what was targeted. Admiral Nelson did it differently. He allowed his commander to make his own decisions. The English ships did not line up, as usual, parallel to their opponents, but drove straight to the opposing line, broke through, causing chaos on the opponent's ship. Each commander under Admiral Nelson could make his own decisions as to how to best attack the enemy. This created a new leadership culture which was based on trust rather than on orders. Virtual teams are more scattered than ships in a sea battle. Therefore, trust and individual responsibility play an even greater role for the motivation and implementation of a strategy.

The Art of Building Trust

As you have already read in a previous chapter, trust has two sides:

First, trust your team members personally and second, trust in their ability and experience. The sympathy factor plays an important role in developing a personal trust. We tend to trust people who have similar values. When this happens, the chemistry seems to be right, and intuitively we like the person. It is therefore very important that people in virtual teams can show their personal values. Allow ample time for your team members to get to know each other and the values of the other person. This allows them to bond at a deep, personal level. This alone, however, rarely suffices.

In order to establish a deep professional trust, it helps for the team to overcome a conflict situation. In his book *The Five Dysfunctions of a Team*,[7] the American management expert Patrick Lencioni describes five "killer factors" for a team performance. If you flip each of these to the positive counterpart, they automatically become the success factors for each team.

Illustration 4: The five Dysfunctions of a Team from Patrick Lencioni

Lencioni represents the five dysfunctions or "killer factors" of a team in the form of a pyramid.

The base of the pyramid is trust - or the absence of trust - as the foundation for everything. In order for grow trust and become resilient, the team has to endure conflicts. Fortunately, confidence increases after every successful conflict. You have already read in this book about how executives can succeed in creating a culture which tolerates – even encourages – making mistakes.

Creating this type of culture is about encouraging people to take calculated risks and being willing to support them if things go wrong. This is the key to innovation. It is important not to blame them for setbacks, but instead to ask what can be learned from the experience. What this means in virtual teams is that no one should accuse or blame another person by email or messaging for mistakes which have been made. Instead, encourage both parties to come together and invite them to a personal conversation in which they can discuss what has been learned from the situation.

In order to resolve conflicts on a lasting basis, wise leadership is necessary. The "inquisitive" style of communication from Peter M. Senge,[8] which we discussed in Chapter 7, is important for effective leadership. Do not be naïve:

Virtual teams must develop a foundation to deal with conflicts. Trust is the most important. Intercultural competence and an "inquisitive" communication style are also necessary.

Conflicts always happen. They cannot be totally avoided. Different working styles, different personalities, and different priorities alone create the potential for conflict.

For example, imagine that you have on your team one person who finds it important to keep a strict appointment schedule. You have yet another person on your team who finds it more important to create and maintain interpersonal relationships but being on time to meetings or meeting deadlines is not as high a priority. This will, over time, cause conflicts.

Intercultural factors also play a significant role on virtual teams and should not be underestimated or ignored. In some cultures, tasks count more than relationships - in others it is the other way round. This is just one example of many possible intercultural conflicts. I would like to recommend Erin Meyer's *The Culture Map*,[9] already mentioned, to better understand intercultural conflicts. It is very helpful for team leaders and the entire team to know the eight dimensions of cultures. It is thus possible to classify where the cause of the respective intercultural conflict may lie. Through these types of resources you can find specific solutions.

Method:
Learn how to distinguish professional, personal and intercultural conflicts. In the understanding of intercultural conflicts, for example, *The Culture Map* by Erin Meyer

Not all conflicts have their roots in character or cultural differences. It may also be that some team members avoid taking responsibility. Or that certain team members want to exercise power and try to dominate their peers. Another situation which may lead to conflicts is if team members lose sight of their goals. Or if they do not identify as strongly with their goals as they may have initially claimed.

To be a strong team in the long run, all these conflicts need to be resolved. Here, again, the "inquisitive" communication style helps to identify the source of the conflicts. The better you understand what drives people and their behavior, the easier it will be to solve the conflict. Conflicts escalate when people stubbornly hold onto their position instead of changing perspective and opening themselves to the needs and intentions of the other team members. If the team members manage, however, to come together and solve the conflict, their trust in each other will grow and deepen.

In virtual teams, commitment and individual responsibility are encouraged primarily through interlinked goals. You encourage individual responsibility in that you allow your team members both to set their own annual targets and to have the freedom to make their own decisions. In addition, these annual goals have to be dependent on other team members and their goals. I described this in detail in Chapter 4.

Where team members themselves assume responsibility, they are also capable of creating conflicts and, as a result, are able to exercise a healthy degree of group pressure. The decisive factor is always the team culture. Where tolerance for making mistakes and an "inquisitive" communication style prevail, and where the team leader is an excellent role model, team performance automatically increases.

The Typical Four Phases of Virtual Teams

Maintaining high levels of commitment in virtual teams is not always easy. The team members work in different places and often there are different organizational levels. It is important to establish how strategic decisions will be communicated to all team members at all locations and at all levels. And, as we have already mentioned, it is important to link individual goals to the goals of other team members and, of course, to the team goal. Emails are often used as the medium to announce decisions to the team members, but this alone is not sufficient to keep everyone on board. It is also important to explain the decisions that have been made during telephone or video conferences in order to give team members the opportunity to ask questions.

It is also important that everyone has the same level of information at all times. The monthly conference with the extended team is an excellent way to keep everyone informed. Allowing for comments or questions at the end of the conference help to involve everyone and give everyone the chance to voice their opinions. Decisions will only be supported and implemented at all levels if you have given everyone the opportunity to ask questions and provide feedback.

Having a single, clear goal for the entire team helps enormously to produce results. In Bernd's team the goal is clear to everyone: The homeless earthquake victims need new houses before the win- *Maintaining high commitment over a long period of time is especially challenging in virtual teams.* ter sets in. This objective is the number one priority. Everything else is secondary to this goal. Teams with such clearly defined goals have a much easier time focusing, setting other priorities, measuring the progress of the project, and engaging with full force. It is also true here: Trust is the basis of everything. It is the one common denominator bonds together all of the resources and activities of the team. Trust, however, is always in danger of being violated. It is not automatically retained once it has been won. It has to be earned time and time again.

Every team - whether present or virtual - goes through certain phases in its development. A number of authors have described these phases scientifically. A classic you may be familiar with is Bruce Tuckman's Four Phase Model.[10] It was first published in 1965 and became known by the names of its four development phases: "Forming, Storming, Norming, Performing." The model can also be applied to all team development, especially the unique development of virtual teams.

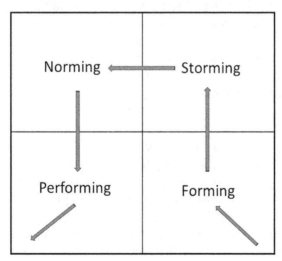

Illustration 5: Bruce Tuckman's Forming Storming Norming Performing (Four-Phase) Model

In the first phase, **Forming**, trust is established on the basis of how we perceive the other person and what we assume about their personality. Because on virtual teams, team members don't usually know each other at the beginning of a project, a workshop can provide the basis for the beginning of trust. Where this is not possible, the personal and professional lifeline exercise should be done for all team members during a video conference.

Bruce Tuckman's classic Four Phase Model can also be applied to virtual teams. Virtual teams are still trying to avoid the conflict phase. Or they want to resolve conflicts by email.

Some teams never leave this first Forming phase. They remain in the comfort zone, polite to each other, but they never realize their full potential. Tuckman observed that only about half of all teams are involved in real discussions about the resolution of conflicts. Only by doing this, can they enter the next phase, the phase of Storming. This is even more extreme in virtual teams. Team members avoid conflicts either completely or try to resolve them by email.

At this point in the development of his team, the team leader plays a decisive role. He should be accessible at all times, communicate intensively both individually with individual team members as well as with the entire team, and he should be able to recognize and call out conflicts. For example, if he realizes that through email communication, a conflict is escalating, he should immediately intervene and draw attention to the situation. The team leader does not need to know the solution to the conflict, but he should ensure that the conflicting parties talk to each other by telephone or in a video conference. While doing this, the team leader should show understanding and openness. Through his own behavior, he signals to the team that it is important to be open and understanding with each other.

The third phase, the **Norming** phase, is about roles and processes. Processes are important but only the basis for the success of the team. True peak performance is created where people are inspired, where they trust each other, and where they give everything they need to succeed. Efficient processes are not a goal unto itself; they are the means to a goal. Norming is best done in virtual teams by transferring responsibility to individual team members. In Bernd's team, Stella is the key figure for the stage of norming.

Watch out, trap!

Conflicts in virtual teams escalate extremely quickly when they are emailed. The Teamchef should have the e-mail traffic in mind and in the event of a conflict make sure that the participants talk in a telephone or videoconferencing.

While the team leader is crucial in the first two phases of team development, he should have less daily influence during the third and fourth phases. During the third and fourth phases, the team leader should modify his communication style. At this time, he should give even fewer instructions and see his role as being more motivating, keeping an eye on the big picture and encouraging the development of individual team members.

Psychologists have found that in a somber and controlled state of consciousness, we can only get a maximum of 60% of our potential. Only in a state of enthusiasm and inspiration can we give 100%. That is why, in the last phase, the **Performing** phase, when the team's maximum performance is important, one of the team leader's most important tasks is to inspire his team.

Regular, structured communication sets the foundation for excellence. At the crucial moment, the commitment is there and new ideas emerge.

In our story, Bernd instinctively trusted his team and was ready to risk his reputation. This risk was rewarded. He was able to see how a top team finds a solution for absolutely every problem. This is Performing. He created the prerequisites for this by providing regular structured communication. At the decisive moment, his people were passionate about the project and reaching their goal. Because of this, they understood the challenges confronting them, and they came up with creative, constructive ideas for the solution.

In a climate of trust, the positive expectations of everyone on the team automatically rise. You come to a point where you believe: With this team, everything is possible! The course is set for outstanding performance and exceptional results.

Part III

Culture

Chapter 9

Virtual Power Teams Can Quickly React to Changes and Take Advantage of Opportunities and Trends

The sunrise was gorgeous. Bernd looked up from the iPad on his lap and looked out the airplane window. Thin clouds lay beneath them like a violet ocean, touched by the first rays of the sun. On the horizon, the violet turned into a bright red. Behind it, one could see the first tiny piece of the rising sun. Bernd was on his way to Munich to visit the biennial trade fair for Architecture, Building Materials and Systems. He hoped to discover new trends and make some interesting contacts.

He hoped to retire to a quiet corner at 11:00 a.m. He was planning a video conference with Anne and Edwin, the junior professor from China, who worked for the MOOC in New York and who, with his team of students, developed the idea to use the new building materials. Bernd had brought Edwin into the extended project team. Now, he wants to find out how the new building materials are working out.

The morning went well. Bernd made his way through the crowds in the exhibition halls. The colorful activity at the attractively designed stands, the many conversations, the hostesses giving out flyers, all the colors, lights, and faces made him curious and aroused his desire for new projects.

Bernd visits a trade fair for architecture and building materials in Munich. Thanks to the independent work of his team, he finally has more time for new contacts and new ideas.

At 11:00 a.m., Bernd is sitting in an armchair in the café area with a fresh coffee in his hand and he starts the WebEx to talk to Anne and Edwin. "Good evening Anne, good evening Edwin, how are you?"

Anne replied, "Good morning, Bernd! I am fine. I am working from home today. We have exciting news for you."

"Good morning Bernd," said Edwin. He sounded calm and reserved. "I am delighted, and I am honored to be speaking with you personally. After many discussions in the expanded team, I can tell you today where we are with the new materials and how they will affect our plans. "

"Outstanding! Today, I am concerned about the completion date of the houses with the new materials. How does our time schedule look?"

"We have made great progress with local builders," said Anne. "Claude, Pilar, Edwin and some of his colleagues and students from the MOOC have been supporting us intensively. Since Edwin has coordinated all the talks, I suggest that he also present our results."

"Excellent," said Bernd. "The virtual stage belongs to you, Edwin."

"First of all, thank you, Bernd, for letting me be the head of the virtual sub-team for the integration of the new building materials," Edwin began. "We will do our utmost to speed up construction."

"I'm glad," said Bernd, smiling. "Welcome on board! I hope you enjoy the work, and I wish you all the best."

"Okay thanks! I've been leading my own virtual team for several weeks now," Edwin said. "We have already had several conferences, and we've managed to speed up the process. In the beginning, we met in in a large round with Claude and Pilar, as well as the chief engineer and construction site coordinator of the construction company. At this point, my core team consists of the engineer and the three MOOC students who won the prizes. Their plans were already included in the final blueprints for the houses. From time to time, Anne helps us coordinate with government agencies. But she is not a permanent member of our team."

Bernd speaks with Edwin, a Chinese associate professor and a new team member, under whose leadership innovative building materials have been developed. The first results have been positive.

Bernd nodded contentedly and took a sip of coffee.

"Together with the three students, I have developed a detailed plan that has been reviewed by the chief engineer and is being tested on site," continued Edwin. "It's a long story, but in short we believe that the houses can be finished by the middle of December. We would then be able to meet your deadlines, Bernd. In order to be 100 percent sure, however, the test buildings would have to be finished first. Only then will we know whether all our calculations are correct and the buildings are resilient."

"Apparently, a lot of progress is being made without me having to get involved. This is great! And if the government still knows who am I, it's even better!" Bernd joked. "Speaking of the government, Anne, do you have any new information about the governmental crisis?"

"Well, Bernd, I wanted to wait until after we talked today, so that I knew what Edwin had to say. Tomorrow I will report to the Minister on our progress, and I will inform him that the houses will most likely be finished in mid-December. On the condition that the test buildings are a success, of course.

"Very well," said Bernd. "Edwin, would you please report on the current plan at the extended team conference next Wednesday? I would like everyone to be up to date. Excellent work so far!"

Bernd closed WebEx, stood up and felt a burst of energy. Yes, indeed, it was true: If you find the right people, bring them together, and give them the freedom to individually take responsibility, everything is possible. He could hardly believe that everything was running so smoothly and quickly, without him having to intervene or put people under pressure. This project was more satisfying and pleasant than any project he had ever worked on before. Relieved and exuberant, he continued through the exhibition halls in search of possible strategic partners for the future.

The next Wednesday Bernd was sitting in his office in Hamburg. The rain drops mingled as they ran down the large windows, and they blurred the view of the large cranes on the other side of the Elbe. Despite the murky day, Bernhard's thoughts were crystal clear: What can our team do to accomplish even more and to finish even sooner? At the fair in Munich, Bernd had seen many new, innovative ideas for smart houses, but they were too expensive for Transmontania. What simpler, more efficient methods could be developed? If the extended team put their heads together, Bernd knew that they would be able to find solutions.

With this in mind, Bernd started WebEx. As soon as he logged in as an organizer, he saw that some members of the extended team were already in the conference.

"Hello, everyone!" Bernd wrote in the chat.

He started the conference punctually at 11:00 a.m.

"A warm welcome to everyone! Today is our fourth conference in the expanded team and we have already come up with many tangible results. You all have really done some outstanding work! As usual, everyone from the core team will tell us where they are in their progress. By doing so, we all will get an overview of how the project is going. If there are questions from the extended team, please ask them in the chat. We will answer your questions at the end. Today, Edwin's contribution is also on the agenda. He will report on the progress made in the use of the new building materials. So, let's go!"

The members of the core team reported on the current status of their target. It was a combination of hard factors about the project and soft factors, such as self-discipline and the integration of external partners. The agenda was just as they had agreed upon in their workshop with Paul.

The efforts for the soft factors were already paying off. One of the most obvious and beneficial rewards from this was the extended team. The "Buddy System" from Kurt Faller,[11] which Linda had introduced to integrate new team members, worked perfectly. Likewise, it proved to be the case that important partners attended some of the regular conferences. Thus, the gravitational force in the team was maintained, although geographically, the team members were further apart than ever before.

Now it was Edwin's turn. "Hello everybody! I am honored to be able to present the results of my work to you. I am an assistant professor in New York, but I also spend a lot of time in my home country of China. For our project here, I lead a sub-team of the award-winning MOOC students and local contact persons in Transmontania to integrate the new materials. First of all, on behalf of my team, I would like to thank Claude and Pilar for their great support. The two gave us many suggestions, shared their experiences with us and linked with important people."

Edwin continued, "Linda has also taken on the task of introducing new members to our project. She explains our goals and purpose to them, so that they can understand what we do and why we do it. Many thanks also to Stella, whose excellent document management makes our ability to collaborate much easier.

With the new sub-teams, the network has grown considerably. This fosters innovation and new ideas. One of these new ideas is to equip the houses with inexpensive solar roofs.

"As you all know, we have opted for new materials in 3-D printing to speed up the construction progress. We are still in the test phase, while the construction work continues uninterrupted." Edwin continued with a detailed report on the milestones of the plan and all they needed to complete the test phase successfully. The first comments and questions were coming in the chat box.

"We have now activated a large network," Edwin said. "The members of my team are talking to various suppliers and potential partners. And from this network yesterday came a whole new idea! One of our students reported that cheap solar roofs in China are on the rise. The whole thing is not yet very well known, but our network has managed to get some figures and calculate what the installation would cost and what efficiency gains would be achieved by solar roofs."

"Interesting!" Bernd was astonished.

"Our assessment is that the solar roofs, especially in the remote areas of Transmontania, would see to it that the government would have much less to invest in the reconstruction of the electricity grid. We therefore propose to take up this trend and at least to equip some of the houses with solar roofs. On the basis of figures from China, we have sketched a business plan. Regarding the funding, with Anne's help we could go directly to the government."

"Why didn't I think of that?" said Claude.

"If we can build the solar roofs as cheaply as in China," Edwin said, "we save not only building costs, but also operating costs. That should be very attractive to the government. "

"Extremely exciting," said Pilar. "I can't stop wondering if that might not be something for South America."

"And for Africa," Linda added radiantly.

"What are the next steps?" Bernd asked.

"I am sending the entire business plan to the core team," explained Edwin. "I'm looking forward to feedback from Claude and Pilar and, of course, from you, Bernd. Once we have considered your feedback, Anne and I will present the plan to the government. Bernd, you should be at this meeting, too, so that the matter has sufficient weight."

"I'll gladly give feedback, of course," said Bernd. "And I would also like to take part in the meeting. At the same time, Edwin, I would like you to continue to be in charge here. Perhaps we really have something here, which could be interesting for all emerging countries."

The team decides to add the solar roofs. Edwin is in charge of developing a business plan. After this, they want to get the government on board. This solution could save a lot of money.

"Please keep me informed," Claude said. "I am active in a great many networks in the construction industry. New materials and methods are always a big issue. We might be a real trendsetter here."

Bernd was enthusiastic. Just a few days ago, he'd shattered his head about how to build faster and more efficiently. Now the ideas were bubbling. They are already in the process of developing a business plan for solar roofs. What the advanced team did through the networks of each member, surpassed all his expectations. So many creative ideas were being discussed without him having to be directly involved, and yet everything was moving exactly in the direction he wanted.

After one week Bernd received an email from Anne which invited him to a conference with the Minister of Energy and Development, the highest-ranking officer for infrastructure development and the director of the state energy company. The aim of the conference was to fix the final completion date for the houses and to discuss the business plan for the solar roofs. The financing and the necessary permits were also to be discussed. From week to week, it became more exciting now! And the team did more and more. Bernd knew intuitively that he could still build a lot in Asia. And he felt grateful for his wonderful team. Yes, he was becoming more grateful every single day. The team was constantly discovering new trends, and because of the high individual responsibility and motivation they could be put their ideas into practice almost immediately.

Virtual Power Teams are able to React Quickly to Trends

Virtual teams are inherently beneficial when it comes to developing rapidly and picking up new trends. If the team culture is right, then the ideas start bubbling up and new trends can be picked up and integrated very quickly. What makes virtual teams so strong?

First of all, there is the difference in the team. If the team members are scattered across different continents, time zones and cultural areas, they also have very different perspectives. Being multi perspective is, according to creativity research, a decisive factor for coming up with new ideas and being innovative. In addition, the more the team members are scattered, the more access they have to networks and thus different information, new trends, and achievements. When different cultures blend in the team, that also makes it creative. The team members bring their understanding of markets and customer needs on different continents. This makes the perspective much broader. Added to this is a very practical advantage: Multicultural teams have access to information in many languages, both online and offline.

If the team culture is healthy, above all, there is individual responsibility and the team members have the feeling that they can assess situations and make their own decisions about them. This, in turn, makes a team eager to reach its goals and more willing to experiment with new things to achieve these goals. The team *Diversity in virtual, multicultural teams encourages creativity. There is access to information in many languages. Together with a strong sense of individual responsibility, innovation grows and new ideas develop.*

members take the initiative, use their personal networks to gather new ideas, and to bind other partners on their own. By the time team members present their ideas to the larger team, they often already have results to report on. This makes it easier for the team to understand the ideas and faster for the larger team to make decisions. In Bernd's project, there is an extended leadership team. This includes all project staff who have distinguished themselves through outstanding achievements. Like Edwin, you get the chance to manage virtual sub-teams and to involve other partners and suppliers.

In hierarchical organizations, for example, globally active groups, the extended leadership team consists of those who report directly to the members of the management team. In smaller organizations, on the other hand, the trend is increasingly that the entire project work is done by self-organizing teams with flat hierarchies. Whatever the initial situation, it is crucial to increase the reach of the virtual team in order to capture and integrate new trends. The further the sensors of the virtual team reach into different networks, the easier it to learn about new trends and innovations, which can be implemented quickly.

This is precisely the goal: innovation. Fast innovation. The question is: what promotes rapid innovation and ensures short innovation cycles? How can trends be detected even earlier and integrated more quickly into projects? In my experience, there are three key factors for rapid innovation:

1. Team structure

2. Communication culture

3. Team culture, in particular performance culture

These three factors are closely related. Where they work together, new trends can be picked up quickly and innovations can emerge.

Team Structure: Traditional or Flat Hierarchies?

In virtual teams, increasingly flat organizational structures are emerging. There is a team leader who calls the team together and organizes the initial team funding. What sets the team's agenda, however, and how it evolves evolutionarily today, depends to a large extent on the entire team. In flat hierarchies, there is no middle management. Everyone reports to the few top managers. This is a model particularly suited to small and medium-sized enterprises (SMEs). In Germany and Western Europe, it is a trend for SMEs to completely eliminate entire hierarchical levels. Of course, it saves costs to forego superfluous management levels, but the greatest advantage is the higher speed of innovation. Companies with flat hierarchies are faster on the market with key projects. They decide more quickly, have a better flow of information and, as a rule, have more committed employees.

Fast, proactive innovation is a question of the team structure, the communication culture, and the team culture. Flat hierarchies tend to be much more innovative.

Surprisingly, SMEs are increasingly focusing on flat hierarchies. An Internet giant like Google is almost completely flat. At Google, there are partial teams with more than 150 people reporting directly to a single senior vice president. The flat structure allows for quick decisions and almost immediate feedback in both directions. The ideal climate for innovation! In such flat hierarchies, completely different reward systems are necessary. At Google, the payment is strictly based on performance, or rather, on the value of an individual's contribution to corporate objectives.

Communication Culture:

Transparency and the Principle of "Followers"

Transparency is everything if you want a good flow of communication and committed employees. Not only do the strategic objectives have to be clear to everyone in the team, but all of the team members should have an active role in defining these goals! Flat hierarchies favor rapid decision-making. There are not so many people who have to agree to a single decision. But for the decision-making to work, total transparency is necessary.

All strategic decisions and their justifications must be publicly known. Usually, important decisions are always made in a synchronous format, typically during a telephone or video conference. This is the only way to ensure that all team members are always behind the team's goals and initiatives, and that all external parties are involved.

Many successful and innovative companies, such as W. L. Gore, are now organizing their project work according to the principle of "followers." Projects are no longer pushed from above, but everyone in the company can start a project and advertise for followers. Individual employees are therefore looking for new ideas in their network, they are researching and looking for fellow employees with whom they can present their concept to others in the company. The better an idea, the higher the probability that others are willing to follow. Everyone in the company makes their own decisions about who they want to follow and which projects they are willing to commit to. The projects which find the most followers will be financed by the company. The number of followers also determines how much management responsibility the project leader will be given. For example, Terri L. Kelly, the CEO of W. L. Gore, is simply the person in the company with the most followers.

In the follower principle, not only the brilliant ideas and concepts are the deciding factors. An employee must also demonstrate the ability to inspire and lead other people. Sometimes, this leadership position is shared between two people: the one is the creative genius and the other more the business leader. Famous examples of such successful tandems are Bill Gates and Paul Allen or Steve Jobs and Steve Wozniak.

In the "followers" principle, projects are no longer top-down. Everyone in the company can advertise their ideas and initiatives to gain followers. The best ideas are determined by those with the most followers.

In virtual teams with flat hierarchies, people come together and organize themselves through individual responsibility. They communicate and find solutions without the Team leader having to intervene each time. For self-organization to work well in the long term, there should be structured group forums that allow people to share, support, or brainstorm creatively. The project management method "Scrum" even provides for a daily conference to start the day. Each team member quickly realizes what their focus is today and who can help them in their work. Often, ideas are already being exchanged at such conferences. In small teams with about five people, a quarter of an hour at the start of the day is enough to come together and share some creative ideas. This method can even work in big teams.

With some internet companies in the Silicon Valley, there is the rule that on one day per week employees should be free to explore their own ideas and projects. The companies give the employees rooms in which they can do their research, test their new ideas, and inspire others in the company. Now you can say that this is typical of Silicon Valley, where product innovations depend very much on the creativity, expertise and productivity of each individual employee. This approach, however, also proves successful in traditional industries because innovation is the key to survival. Self-organization, self-responsibility and the principle of "followers" are taken over by many companies, regardless of their size and product field. It pays off.

Team Culture:
Free and Self-Determined Brings Top Performance

The third decisive factor for rapid innovation is the team culture. This is about values.

Virtual collaboration allows for great freedom. Each person may choose when and where they would like to work. As a result, freedom automatically becomes a core value of any virtual team. In my experience, freedom happens automatically. The team leader does not have to talk about it or officially implement it. It should be a given. In virtual teams, it is far better to grant a great deal of freedom and to measure the employees' results rather than measuring how many hours they have been working. In addition to freedom, autonomy and self-realization are important values in self-organizing virtual teams. The basic principle of virtual teams with flat hierarchies is that top experts work most productively if they are directly involved in the decision-making process and are not constantly monitored by "top". The role of leadership in virtual teams is far from the traditional top-down approach. Managers are now more "enablers" than anything else. Their quality is measured by the extent to which they succeed in inspiring and motivating people.

In flat hierarchies, career is no longer a great motivation factor because there are hardly any formal leadership positions to fill. Much more tempting is the opportunity to quickly take on responsibility on projects and to have appropriate decision-making competences. In Bernd's team, Edwin took advantage of this opportunity. The subject of new building materials is now

Freedom is almost always one of the core values of every virtual team, since each team member has the freedom to choose when and where they will work. Working independently is often a higher value for many than having a traditional career path.

"his." Being an integral part of high-speed innovation and an intensive exchange of ideas is often more motivating than aspiring to become "boss" in a formal hierarchy.

There is a close link between self-determination and innovation. Innovative research says that innovation is usually the result of a spontaneous exchange of ideas. Highly innovative companies, such as Google or Apple, consciously make a point of informally bringing people together as often possible so that they have the opportunity to exchange creative thoughts and ideas. The many cafés and lounge-like areas in Silicon Valley companies are not just a luxury; they exist to promote the informal and unplanned creative exchange. Spontaneity and "controlled chance" are certainly a good approach. I believe, however, that the structured communication processes of virtual teams can also stimulate creativity. It is necessary to set up appropriate slots at regular conferences to allow informal discussions. You have already read a lot about these structures in Part II of this book.

Not only cultural differences, but also self-determination is, according to innovation research, a decisive factor for the rapid development of many new, creative ideas. Structured communication can also promote innovation.

Some companies that I have advocated follow a very exciting approach: they rely on "virtual cafés." Team members agree to informally meet via video conference with a cup of coffee or tea in their hands to simply converse with each other. It is important that everyone has access to a digital whiteboard to write down and keep track of ideas. For most video conferencing applications, a whiteboard is included. Whether such formats ultimately lead to innovation, ultimately depends less on the technology, but on the extent to which those in leadership positions recognize how useful these informal approaches can help team creativity and innovation and how much they encourage their use. Of course, you can also invite a network partner to a "virtual café". Thus, the creative exchange becomes even more diverse - and the results may become even more interesting. A virtual team has an unbeatable advantage over a live team, because it is much easier to invite interesting, innovative people from the outside to the meetings. In a "normal" team this just wouldn't be possible without having to fly the visitors in.

In "virtual cafes" team members agree on meeting for a coffee or tea by videoconference so they can brainstorm and exchange ideas in a relaxed setting. They write down their ideas on a virtual whiteboard. Guests are allowed to attend, and they greatly enrich the discussion.

You can also learn from the open-source movement in the IT sector. Here, too, the principle is usually that someone initiates a project and "follower" searches for it. These edit and refine the open source code, which is put online by the initiator of the project. Companies can take a look at this, for example, by integrating important partners into a project virtually and allowing them to work out individual steps independently. High-speed innovation and extraordinary success are possible where people can enjoy freedom, experience autonomy and realize themselves and their dreams.

Chapter 10

Whoever Promotes Diversity Instead of Combating It, Raises Potential

The autumn holidays with the family were very relaxing. Bernd spent ten days on Tenerife with his wife and daughter. Blue skies and sunshine gave him energy, quite different from the dreary weather in Hamburg. During the entire ten days on Tenerife, there was only one day where there was a short but violent downpour. Perhaps it was the last remnants of a storm far out at sea? Soon afterwards a magnificent rainbow appeared over the Atlantic.

Every day, Bernd played tennis with his daughter, Lena, and then took long beach walks with Wiebke, during which the two conversed intensely. He had promised both Wiebke and Lena not to read a single email during the holidays. If anything urgent should occur which requires his immediate attention, Bernd asked his team to contact him on his cell phone.

Going without any digital communication was refreshing and rejuvenating. But as the days passed, however, Bernd's curiosity grew. He wanted to know how things were going in Transmontania. The team had made two important innovative decisions shortly before Bernd's departure: the new building materials

On vacation Bernd did not read any emails. After he returned, however, he saw that the Asian director wants Bernd's signature on the amended contracts. No big deal, Bernd thinks.

and the solar roofs. Bernd really wanted to know how these two things were affecting their timetable and the quality of the results.

Bernd slept most of the way on the return flight. He decided he would wait to retrieve his emails after landing in Hamburg. Once he reached the baggage claim, he could wait no longer! He took out his iPhone and quickly scrolled through the new emails. His daughter had to pull him by the sleeve, so he did not miss one of her heavy suitcases on the baggage belt.

At first glance, there appeared to have been no emergencies during the ten days. There were a few new emails from Edwin about the first experiences with the solar roofs and the new building materials. In some of the emails had the subject line "decision needed." Bernd opened these emails first.

When they reached the car park, Wiebke offered to drive, so that Bernd could continue to read through his emails. Normally, she was not quite so generous, but the beautiful days in Tenerife had brought them closer together, and she realized how important this project is for Bernd. Out of gratitude for her understanding and in the attempt to extend the vacation just a little longer, Bernd offered to cook dinner for her this evening. "Besides," he joked, "Maybe it will win me some more points for the next time I screw up!"

Wiebke laughed and said, "Keep on dreaming!"

As far as the emails were concerned, new tools and new suppliers were needed for the new materials. Decisions had to be made. Bernd had agreed in principle for the team members to spend additional money as long as they remained within the budgetary restrictions. It looked, however, as if the Asian construction company wanted to see Bernd's signature on the new contracts. "Okay, we'll get that done quickly," thought Bernd, and he asked Edwin to organize a videoconference with the manager of the construction company and his most important employees.

Two days later the video conference was on while Bernd himself was on the road. There was an unexpected problem on a construction site in Germany, and he needed to meet the site manager on short notice. Bernd had agreed to the meeting only reluctantly, knowing that this would mean that he would have to do the video conference with the Asian construction company from his car. At 10:30 a.m., Bernd pulled over at a rest stop on the highway and opened WebEx on his iPhone.

This was far from his first conference on the road, but he was a bit nervous this time. After he started the conference, he could see Anne immediately. She sat in the office of the construction company next to the director of the construction company, an Asian business man of middle age, and two of his closest associates, the chief engineer and the construction site coordinator. Edwin took part in the videoconference from China, this time with a suit and a tie. Bernd had never seen the assistant professor wearing a tie.

"Good evening, everyone together," Bernd began the conference. "I apologize for taking our conference from my car. I have to go to an urgent meeting on one of my construction sites, and there was just no other way. I hope everyone can see and hear me."

"Good morning, Mr. Bernd," the construction manager replied dryly. Bernd was accustomed to the fact that Asians called him "Mr. Bernd", because it was difficult for them to meet foreign business partners with their first names. Normally, it took a long time before they said anything but Bernd.

"I am delighted to discuss the consequences of the last two innovations with you," continued the director. "On the one hand, we are familiar with more efficient technologies that speed up construction. On the other hand, we need to involve new suppliers, train employees and integrate more people into the team. This means more overhead and more costs for us. I would like to talk with you about how we divide these costs."

"So, with all respect, Mr. Director, I had asked Edwin to steer the introduction of the two innovations and do not know what to discuss between us. If I have understood Edwin correctly, then the new materials as well as the solar roofs are ultimately cost neutral, because the productivity gains correspond approximately to the investments. This means that you will invest a bit more now but gain that back as soon as the solar roofs are functioning. Did Edwin not discuss this with you during my vacation?"

During a telephone conference, strong cultural differences between Bernd and the Asian director become apparent. Bernd says that Edwin could have clarified everything with the director.

"Professor Edwin has discussed this with my chief engineer and my construction site coordinator. I am attached to your personal commitment, Mr. Bernd. With regard to this as well as future cooperations."

"Mr. Director, may I tell you a little about me? I used to do what you are proposing with my teams in Germany. I took care of everything myself and signed every bill. Now I'm head of a great virtual team. I trust my team and I delegate important competences, also with regard to the budget, as long as we remain within the agreed framework. Edwin is your contact. And by the way, why do not you actually try that? Give your people more options to make decisions! Then we will actually progress even faster with the project. Believe me, it pays off."

It is scandalous when Bernd gives advice to the Asian director about how he should lead his team. The director puts the project on hold and threatens to end his business relationship with Bernd. Bernd can hardly believe his ears.

While he spoke, Bernd saw Edwin looking irritated at the camera and then lowering his gaze. Anne listened, but seemed alerted.

Bernd felt that he had gone to a muddy ground, but he was not sure why.

Before Bernd could ask, the director had already intervened.

"Reverend Mister Bernd, I'm afraid we will have to postpone a week and consider our business relationship." His voice was frosty. Although he was totally under control, Bernd could see that he was tormented. He could hardly believe his ears.

"What do you mean to postpone a week?" He shouted into the microphone. "We have valid contracts and thousands of people need to move into their homes before winter!"

"We'll be back in a week. Until then, we are interrupting the construction work. The contractual penalties for this are known to us."

"But that's ridiculous!" Bernd shouted. "What's your fucking problem?"

At the moment Bernd saw a personal message from Anne in the chat: "Bernd, please stop pressuring him. If possible, please apologize immediately for interfering in the affairs of the other company. Let us discuss the next steps immediately after the conference."

"Mr. Director," said Bernd in a quiet voice, "If I have offended you in any way, I beg your pardon. I was just glad that we were finally able to speed up the construction work and were on the verge of catching up to our proposed timeline. I regret very deeply that you would like to suspend construction for a week, and I am very sorry if I have caused you to make this decision. I am already looking forward to our next meeting. If there is anything I can do to help you resume the work earlier, please let me know."

"I'll get back to you as soon as we're ready. Goodbye, Mister Bernd."
This ended the conference.

Although it had become cold in the car, Bernd felt his sweat sweating through his shirt. "What's wrong here?" He asked himself. "Why did Edwin not do his job? And why did the engineer and the coordinator not simply bless the matter? "

Bernd stepped out of the car to catch a breath of fresh air. "What just happened?" he asked himself. As soon as he got back into the car, he called Anne on her cell phone.

"Anne, hopefully you have a reasonable explanation for what has just happened?"

"Bernd, I do not know if you are aware of it, but all Asian cultures, especially Transmontania, are very authoritarian. The supreme boss always has the last word and must be involved everywhere. When we enter into cooperations here, it goes strictly according to the hierarchy of who talks with whom. Edwin and I were able to discuss a lot with the chief engineer and the construction site coordinator. But when it comes to investment, the agreement has to be signed by the two bosses. You need to respect this hierarchy and speak directly to the director without involving us. Because you were on holiday, the new contracts have already been delayed. This is not a good sign.

Taking vacations is not as sacred in Asia as in Europe. The real problem here, however, is that you have now given the director advice on how to lead his team better. I am afraid he has interpreted this as a personal criticism. He might just have swallowed it just now, but you publicly criticized him in front of his own people. He has lost his face. In Asia, this is the worst thing that can happen in a conversation."

Anne explains to Bernd why his communication was offensive from the Asian point of view. She explained that in Asia, only the bosses can sign agreements, whereas in Europe this task may be delegated to someone down the line.

"So, what you are saying is that because I gave him some tips, is he now angry and is stopping construction for a week? In addition, he's questioning our entire business relationship and all our contracts?

"Yes, Bernd, that's about it. Look, I also think that he overreacted. This is a large project, and there are potentially a lot more contracts coming. So, my guess is that things will soon calm down. I suggest you ask him for a personal phone call for day after tomorrow. If you would allow, I would like to help you to write an appropriate email for this."

"You know, I'm a German. We're rather direct, and we tend to stick to the facts rather than to worry about what everyone is feeling. But our project is in danger. Therefore, I would like to take you up on your offer."

Bernd drove back onto the highway and started to reflect on what just happened. Why did this problem have to happen right now, as they are all ready for the final sprint? The more people coming onto the team from all over the world, the greater the risk of intercultural misunderstandings.

Anne also finds the reaction of the Asian businessman a bit exaggerated. At the same time, she understands where he is coming from. Bernd realizes that he has underestimated how important intercultural relations are.

"I have to be careful," thought Bernd. "Diversity is obviously a risk. I have to get this risk under control. But how?"

At once he thought of Paul. Probably it was once again time for a telephone call. This man always had an ace up his sleeve. Bernd and Paul arranged to skype on the following evening.

Bernd was still in his office when he started Skype. He had made himself comfortable with his laptop in his seat.

"Good evening, Bernd. Please tell me what all has happened." Paul began. He sounded as fresh as ever.

"So, first of all, my holiday was fantastic! Probably you have also read the reports that we are now slowly catching up the delay? The tests with the new materials were all successful. I thought we were ready to begin the final sprint."

"All the information that I have seen also looks quite like things are going well and about to wrap up."

"That is all well and good, but brace yourself for the latest. I had a phone call with the director of the construction company the yesterday, and I managed to put my foot in my mouth. "

"What happened?"

Bernd told Paul that he wanted to give the Asians a few tips. The director, however, understood this as personal criticism, and he completely overreacted. His subordinates, Anne and Edwin, just sat there and said nothing.

"Oh, I see. That's how it is in Asia, Bernd. It is so important to respect the cultural differences, and you should never criticize anyone in front of the others -- especially not in front of their subordinates. That undermines their authority."

"Yes, yes, Anne explained that to me. The question is what we can do now? Anne suggested that I call the man again privately. She is also willing to help me write the email asking to meet with him."

"That's a good idea. Anne knows how to hit the right tone. As for your team, I would like to propose an intercultural workshop so that something like this won't happen again in the future. In this workshop, you and your team will become familiar with all the different cultures which are represented in the project, and you will learn the

Anne helps Bernd to smooth everything over, and Bernd decides to contact Paul for more advice. Paul proposes that the team do an intercultural workshop to learn more about each other's culture.

most important ways of interacting with each other. It is, by the way, very similar to the personal Lifeline: you just ask people what they are proud of in their culture. You can do this over a video conference, so do not worry about the cost. But make sure that everyone in their culture brings something to show the others - photos or a short video or sing a song."

Diversity as a Challenge and an Opportunity

We live in a time when more than 60% of all business teams are spread over more than one time zone. Often the team members come from different countries and cultures. This is a challenge and an opportunity at the same time. Multicultural teams are important to the future of our planet. I am firmly convinced of this. For the differences between people in companies and teams, the keyword "Diversity" has been established in recent years. There are different aspects of diversity, for example gender, age, or cultural background.

Global virtual teams naturally live diversity, especially with regard to different cultures. On the one hand this is an enrichment, since the different cultural experiences and values also allow for different perspectives. On the other hand, cultural diversity also carries risks, as intercultural conflicts can come to light or simmer under the surface. In this chapter, I would like to show how diversity can be understood and used as an opportunity in virtual teams. If you want diversity on your team, then you should promote it and give it space. This is the basic principle. Cultural and other differences should be allowed to exist and be shown in the team. Let's look at the most important features of diversity and its advantages.

The more diverse a virtual team is, the greater the personal and cultural differences. These differences are not only challenging. They can also be a great source of opportunity. These cultural differences should be openly discussed and shown!

First of all, the topic of *Gender Diversity*. This is about the potential of women in business. One of my success secrets as a manager was that I drastically increased the women's quota on each of my teams. For some teams, especially in the IT sector, I initially had a women's rate of 0 percent and within two years it was 50 percent or more. I just failed with my attempt to increase the men's quota at home – try though I may, I have five daughters. But back to virtual teams.

A healthy mix of men and women in a team ensures more balanced discussions and helps to better understand the needs of customers and stakeholders in the company. In each team, there are also roles that are usually filled by women rather than men. When it comes to multitasking, adhering to rules, or showing empathy, women are generally easier to deal with. When people barely have the opportunity to communicate with one another, women often recognize the problems more quickly. Women are more sensitive to the needs of the others and they can sense when someone in the team feels poorly treated.

Men, on the other hand, are generally more willing to take risks and often have more entrepreneurial spirit. It is important to recognize that there is no better or worse. The right mixture between male and female qualities in the team is important. In my experience, this mixture is what leads to better performances.

A second type of Diversity is in regard to different *Age Groups*. Incorporating people of different ages offers a wealth of opportunities in virtual teams. The technically efficient digital natives and the experienced generation X together with the older generations complement each other well. Mutual mentoring is an approach to build relationships and promote personal development. The very young, for example, can show the elderly how to deal with the Internet, apps, and online tools. In turn, the younger ones can learn a lot from the older ones about strategy and risk management.

The most important form of diversity in virtual teams is undoubtedly *Cultural Diversity*. Often more than 50% of the team members come from different cultures. How to bridge cultural differences and make positive use of them to achieve maximum performance is therefore an important challenge for virtual teams.

Building Bridges Through Intercultural Understanding

I have a very simple metaphor for intercultural management in a team: I compare it with cooking. You need a recipe, a stove, and a pot in which you cook the ingredients. Then, from these different ingredients, you create a tasty dish. The recipe is understanding the different cultures in a team. In addition, it is understanding what dish is to be created together. In other words, it is the gathering of the ingredients. The stove is the energy that we need to transform the ingredients into something new and beautiful. The preparation and stirring of the food is our rituals and structured communication. He who wants to cook should know what he wants to create. In a virtual team, the entire team needs to know what they are going to create.

The first step is to get to know the individual team members with their respective cultural backgrounds. From Chapter 1 you already know the exercise with the professional and personal lifelines. In order to get a better understanding of the cultures involved, you can proceed very similarly.

Intercultural workshops can help virtual, multicultural teams to discover and appreciate diversity. Let people present what they are particularly proud of in their culture.

Instead of representing themselves, in the intercultural workshop the team members represent and present the "lifelines" of their respective cultures. Let all representatives of a country briefly say something about its history, explain typical customs and represent the most important values. Ask each team member to present something from his culture: pictures of places or cultural events, sing or dance a folk song, tell about traditions or something that people in their country are particularly proud of. Music and videos are especially good. They should not only talk about the achievements of the countries that are presented, but also unique or witty traditions or customs. An intercultural workshop is always fun.

Examples of stories from individual countries

Kenya. In Kenya and Uganda, the bridegroom has to pay for his future wife in cows. And not only before the wedding, but for a lifetime, to secure the bride's family. It is tradition that the bridegroom and the father of the bride negotiate a corresponding "contract" for the coming years.

Malaysia. A Polish friend was transferred to Malaysia to manage a team that provides IT services to branch offices around the world. The Malaysian society consists of three large ethnic groups: Malay, Chinese and Indian. With his typical Polish cordiality, my friend went through the offices during the first week and offered his colleagues small pieces of sausage, which he had cut off with a Swiss knife. Most of the staff were friendly but said, "No, thank you." This surprised my friend. Later, a team member got up the courage to explain the situation. The Malays are predominantly Muslims and, therefore, do not eat pork. The Chinese do not eat anything that is cut with a knife. And the Indians were afraid that it might be beef of sacred cows in the sausages, but they were afraid to ask because they didn't want to offend him.

India. The famous patience of the Indians is sometimes problematic when the deadline approaches. Indians like to take their time, and it is almost impossible to rush them. If you ask them to commit to something, Indians will most likely say yes, because it is hard for them to refuse something directly. So, it can be that an Indian says, "Yes, I'll do it by tomorrow," and the task is still not done several days later. The only thing that can help in this situation is to develop a sense of trust and understanding.

Bulgaria. There are some universal body language signals that have the same meaning almost all over the world, but there are exceptions. For example, to shake your head in Bulgaria means "yes" and to nod your head means "no". So, it's the opposite of most places in the world.

Colombia. When Colombians want to point at or show something, they tend to point their noses at it. So, just as in other cultures we use the index finger to point at something, they use the nose.

From all of the workshops I have done over the years, I could tell you many stories about different cultural peculiarities. These workshops are amusing and uplifting. In going through these exercises, the team realizes that cultural differences are exactly that which brings spice into the team and helps it to be unique. But be careful: there are also a lot of prejudices and stereotypes about certain countries and ethnic groups. Make sure that no prejudices dominate, but the team members actually learn something about the different cultures. The key to this is a genuine curiosity and respect. Respect for the different cultures and respect for each other.

Common Goals Fuse Cultures

In order to unite people from different cultures in a team, a common goal is needed. The goal is like a magnet that attracts people from all over the world. In the new business world, more and more people are working on projects which are oriented toward common goals. At the same time, fewer and fewer people work in the "silos" of large companies, where they only assemble small pieces of a puzzle which somehow create a larger business process. The young digital natives are already very open to multicultural teams. They expect that there are clear goals and one can personally develop and have fun on the job. A meaningful contribution to a better world is much more important than traditional career opportunities.

Method:
When you are setting ambitious goals for your team, do not do this alone but work with your team to develop the goals and to explain why these goals are desirable. Ask if your work improves the lives of people and is a response to the challenges of our time.

Let's go back to the cooking metaphor for intercultural bridge building. If we have a stew on the stove, we should stir it from time to time or it will get burnt. In virtual teams, this "stirring" means having regular rituals, in which team members can show how their culture would traditionally react to the given situation. Everyone should have the same opportunity to share anecdotes or aspects of their culture in meetings or in telephone and video conferences. I can only recommend putting cultural issues on the agenda. Reserve a slot during meetings, where team members can talk about the different cultural aspects of the whatever the subject may be.

Intercultural topics should be regularly placed on the agenda. For example, make a timeslot at conferences, where team members talk about their culture.

If more than one person from a specific culture is present, the group should name a speaker to represent them and their respective culture during the meeting. They may perhaps even play a suitable piece of music. It has also proven to be useful when a virtual team also exchanges social media on intercultural topics. For example, the team could have a closed Facebook group where the team members can post their contributions to cultural topics. There may be photos of the Chinese New Year, the Muslim fasting month of Ramadan or the Diwali, the Hindu light festival.

Often misunderstandings are also caused by the different languages in the virtual teams. Different language usage even has an effect if the working language is English.

In English, for example, "not too bad" means that something is "pretty good," just like you say in German "not bad". This type of "double negation," however, is not known in many other European languages. The team members, therefore, may not understand what is meant here. In other cultures, people sometimes say yes and mean no. And when a Briton says "interesting", then that does not necessarily mean that he finds something really interesting. He can also mean "terrible" and not want to say it out of politeness. In multicultural teams, it is important to avoid subtle allusions, double entendres, and implied meanings. These only cause confusion and, for the team members not "in the know," frustration. Be as clear as possible and use the chat function to communicate in writing.

In virtual teams, different cultures melt together, because everyone is working towards a common goal.

In my image of cooking, the stove is the third element to bridge cultural differences. We bridge differences by bringing the different cultures together in one pot and allowing them to melt together, the so-called melting pot. What then comes out is something new and exciting and very unique. We create something that would not have been possible if we had left even just one of the "ingredients," just one of the cultures out of the mix. If everyone realizes this, then they realize how important each team member is to the success of the team. What is created from this melting pot is the character of the team, and this character is also what adds emotion to the team. The team goal is the magnet that pulls the team together, but emotion is what drives a team to an outstanding success. And this emotion comes from the melting pot, from heating the ingredients to get them excited. And this excitement is the element that gives your team power and energy. Make sure the team members have fun and can be proud of who they are and what they have done. Keep the stove hot. In other words, keep the emotion and excitement going to help drive your team to the finish line.

To take the cooking metaphor one step further, recognition is like the spice when cooking. Make sure everyone is seen. This spice goes into the cooking pot, and reinforces the excitement. In the end, everyone should feel appreciated and should feel like a hero. Appreciate the uniqueness of each team member and give them the feeling of being a star. Praise them as much as possible for their contributions, skills or attitudes.

Working with the Culture Map according to Erin Meyer

If you have multicultural teams, you should work with *The Culture Map*. In her book *The Culture Map*,[12] Erin Meyer distinguishes eight dimensions, in which the countries and cultures of the world differ on a flowing scale. These eight dimensions are: communication, performance assessment, conviction, leadership, decision making, trust, criticism and scheduling (see graphic).

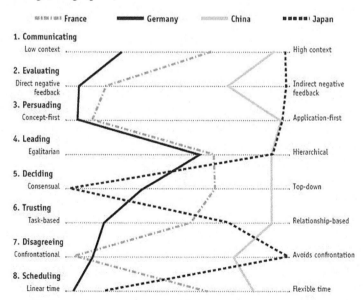

Illustration 6: The eight Dimensions of *The Culture Map* by Erin Meyer

In my experience, leadership (leading), deciding and disagreeing are the neuralgic points in virtual teams. I have already dealt with various leadership styles in the previous chapters. In some hierarchical cultures, for example, it is not customary to contradict the boss in the presence of others. Also, here the boss has to be asked for permission for every important step. The boss is expected to answer all questions of the team. The communication is also hierarchical here, that is, team members have different hierarchy levels, which are not directly related to each other. Information is passed strictly along the command chain.

As you have already read elsewhere, I recommend an egalitarian team culture based on individual responsibility for virtual teams. All team members should make decisions for themselves and find their own solutions - as long as they comply with the agreed upon timetables and budgets. The team members must also be allowed to object in the team. The boss, in turn, should be seriously interested in the views of others. In the team, everyone is talking to everyone, as it is objectively necessary. It does not follow the hierarchy.

The neuralgic points in virtual teams are leadership, decision-making, and criticism. A multicultural team needs its own team culture with regard to these topics.

Now, if you have people from Japan, Korea, India, Russia or other strictly hierarchical cultures in your virtual team, and at the same time, you have team members from Denmark, Sweden, Norway or Australia, so extremely egalitarian cultures, then you should initially be in a synchronous format in order to create a common team culture. I have already described this in a previous chapter.

The team culture is best created on the basis of respect for the cultural backgrounds of each of the team members. Everyone should know and appreciate the advantages and disadvantages of the other cultures. It is best to use stories about the characteristics of the different cultures. Only if the team members are aware of what is unique about each other's cultures does real understanding arise.

As soon as such an understanding of the cultures exists, the team will be able to agree on the team culture to be based on the eight scales described by Meyer. As you already know, I encourage all virtual teams to position themselves more on the egalitarian side. Virtual collaboration naturally requires freedom and individual responsibility. Authority, hierarchy and command are very difficult over long distances. This does mean that once a certain direction for virtual teams has already been set, your job is to help the team go in this direction despite being pulled in other directions.

Let's take a closer look at how decisions are made, what Meyer labels "Deciding." With deciding, the Meyer scale ranges from pure top-down decisions to decisions which are made with complete consensus from everyone.

My recommendation is to reach as much consensus as possible early in the project, for example in a joint work-

In developing your project with your team, try to reach as much consensus as possible. One way might be, for example, in a joint strategy workshop. The team leader should only step in and make a final decision when the team disagrees and come to an impasse.

shop on strategy and objectives. In virtual teams, it is important that all team members be involved in strategic decisions and objectives. Even if later there is a strategic change of focus or a major change which affects the work of the entire team, the team should come together again to reach a joint consensus as how to move forward. The team leader should only make use of a top-down decision when there is not clear consensus from the group. This creates clarity and brings the team back on track.

If the team leader makes a decision, he should be receptive to feedback and be able to revise his decision as the project progresses. This is especially true when things do not go according to plan.

Another intercultural challenge is the way different cultures express criticism. On the Meyer scale, the two extremes are confrontational and avoiding confrontation. As soon as there are team members from cultures which express criticism very differently, conflicts can arise very quickly. This especially occurs in meetings where controversial issues are discussed and it is expected that everyone contributes to the discussion.

I advise virtual teams to make criticism as confrontational as possible in order to make quick decisions. For team members, for example from Japan, China or Saudi Arabia, this is hard to bear. Luckily, there are some tricks to help team members who want to avoid any confrontation, nevertheless, to participate in discussions. For example, make it clear before each discussion that there is always only dissent in the matter and never about the rejection of a person. In some cultures, these two are considered one and the same. A Japanese or Chinese person may feel personally attacked if you criticize his point of view. If this happens, try to increase awareness that it is in fact possible to separate both - as you find in most European cultures.

As a team leader, you should ensure that conferences do not lead to extreme confrontations. Make sure that the discussions are objective and not subjective. If there are difficulties with this, ask your team members to submit their points of view in writing.

Another trick is to avoid the direct clash of different opinions in conferences. Simply ask the team members to submit their positions in writing ahead of time. This gives everyone plenty of time to deal with different opinions and to prepare the discussion. For people from cultures where it is extremely difficult to take criticism, you could even create the possibility that team members post their opinions anonymously. As a team leader, you should also avoid discussing your opinion. Ask everyone else about their opinion. Otherwise, many team members, especially those from authoritarian cultures, will be guided by your point of view.

Team Culture, Yes – Compartmentalization, No

As we have already discussed, over time a team culture emerges, and it begins to override the cultural differences in the team. It is also important to ensure that team culture does not become so strong that it conflicts with the corporate culture. I once had a case in which this happened. I was leading a team of 20 project managers in a corporate organization. We had fantastic figures, and yet my boss called me to the office and accused me of creating a state within the state. He found that my team was too different from the other employees in the company and we should change that. Our very good results did not help me at all. I learned a lot from this situation.

The Team Newsletter

How about a team newsletter that everyone can subscribe to? Through this, outsiders remain informed, get to know their team members better, understand the cultural differences, and develop understanding for their special team culture.

To avoid a negative attitude towards your team from the rest of the company, it is important to stay in regular communication with important stakeholders, including your supervisors and the personnel division.

The corporate culture should be respected first and foremost. Just as you communicate changes and decisions within your team, you should always do the same externally. Let your corporate partners know what your team is doing, where you see them going, and why your team may take a different cultural stand at certain times. Always remain open for feedback from others in the corporation and be prepared to change course if conflicts with the corporate culture arise.

One good idea to help with this is to name ambassadors who represent the team to the outside and regularly communicate with other departments in the company. These ambassadors should take part in corporate events and present the progress of the team. Conversely, you can invite stakeholders to your own project meetings from time to time. By doing this, you avoid the impression that you are pulling a fence around your garden and excluding the others.

Interview with Cemal Osmanovic

Cemal Osmanovic, born in 1958, is the founder and CEO of smile2 GmbH in Schweinfurt as a platform for people who want to continue developing professionally and personally. Today, the platform is one of the market leaders in the field of professional live online seminars in the B2B area in the German-speaking world.

After completing his studies, Cemal Osmanovic led a successful IT service company for 11 years and, starting in 1994, accompanied numerous IT companies as a consultant and entrepreneur coach. In 1999, he sold the company. Together with his co-managing director Rüdiger Sievers, he developed the iTeam system house group by the end of 2008 into the largest IT network company with a total of more than 330 locations and 9,000 employees. By the beginning of 2009, he focused even more on his core themes of training, development, and inspiration for people. With this goal in mind, Cemal Osmanovic founded smile2 GmbH.

Who are you and what do you do? Just describe yourself!

In my youth, I was a professional musician. As someone who is half-turkish, Oriental passion is already in my blood. Nevertheless, I studied mathematics and later computer science. So, I am both an emotional type and a structured computer scientist.

All the important decisions I have made in my life have been value-oriented. My professional mainstays are people who develop and create great things, have power, create lasting benefits and have fun at the job. Therefore, I became an entrepreneur at a very early age and have always remained so.

I am currently running smile2, a market-leading company for professional live online seminars on all non-professional topics, such as marketing, online marketing, communication and rhetoric, time and self-management and, above all, leadership and sales. Personally, I am an expert for success. This means that I support people in finding the right goals for themselves, which guarantee success and quality of life for a long time and whose implementation I also like to accompany.

This is done either through open seminars or for entrepreneurs and executives in a 1: 1 weekend coaching. This is what I call "Entrepreneurial Clarity."

What are the main technologies for collaboration in virtual teams?

To properly understand my answer to this question, let me briefly summarize what is, according to my philosophy, most important in a company. First, does the company have a tangible spirit or culture which can be sensed by everyone who comes into contact with the company? Is everyone involved with the company aware of this spirit, and do they act in congruence with it? Second, is there a clearly defined goal and a daily strategy? Third, are there best practices and successful business models to learn from and incorporate into the company? And is there a target group that really needs these products? Finally, communication, communication, and once again communication!

Virtual teams need to communicate clearly, and they need to be more sensitive to what other team members are saying in order to avoid misunderstandings.

In a modern organization, all of these elements should be supported and carried out by not only the employees in the regional offices but also by the virtual teams. Of course, with virtual teams there are challenges to overcome, especially in regard to communications. Communications need to be even clearer than in teams that meet in person, because it is more difficult to read the body language or to directly ask other team members about something than when the group is in the same room. We need to be more acutely aware and sensitive in virtual teams to avoid misunderstandings. As a prime example, do not carry on conflicts or disagreements through emails. This rule should apply to conventional teams as well, but the temptation to do this is even greater in virtual teams. And finally, a clear documentation of all results and decisions is even more important for virtual teams.

What technologies or apps do you recommend, depending on the size of the company?

Since the customer should always be the focus of our interest in a modern company, a CRM system – especially the willingness to use it - is absolutely essential. For excellent transparency and effective communication, it is necessary to have a synchronized portal, such as a wiki, a web-based project management software such as Trello or the like. More important than the tool itself is the fact that this tool is consistently and uniformly used by all parties involved, and that it is so perfectly structured that all relevant information is easy to find quickly. Otherwise, no one will use it!

In virtual teams, of course, it is important to have ways to bring the team together as a substitute for being physically in the same geographical place. There are modern solutions for this using software which allows the team to see and hear each while conferencing. One such program for this is Skype. It is important that the team has a high-quality video conferencing system with a very good camera quality, an absolutely disturbance-free sound transmission, and screen sharing, so that the participants in meetings can work together, for example, to create a Mindmap. We are currently using Adobe Connect as an online seminar company.

What are your experiences with virtual teams?

I would say good to very good! I can start with the fact that when I work with virtual teams, I get better more highly qualified people, because I am not limited to choosing people from my geographical location. And somehow,

In virtual teams, you have to find a substitution for people meeting in person. In my opinion, this can be easily solved through modern technology and software developed for this purpose.

I feel that with virtual teams, the employees are more hungry and flexible in their thinking than team members who get up and go to work every day in the same place with the same people and sometimes fall into the same old trot. It can also be that with a virtual team, I subconsciously lead differently. I strive to communicate more clearly, because I know that the communication channels are more limited than with a convention team.

Which of your achievements as a leader and entrepreneur are you particularly proud of?

That I managed to become market leader in all three companies that I founded and raised. Admittedly, this is not always measurable. But that aspect is not as important to me. Just to know that we are one of the market leaders in our field makes me proud. I am not so much about being the absolute number one. I am about creating something great, something essential, something that has importance for many people.

As for myself, I once again realize how important it is to create a tangible company spirit and philosophy which reflects our values and to live both of these in my company. I want this on the one hand, because I want to live this philosophy intensively. On the other hand, I also want this because in times when competition is so high, this gives the company a unique positioning on the market. With this philosophy, I have managed to create three successful companies, two of which I sold for a considerable amount of money. This success proves, in my opinion, that we were on the right track.

Successfully founding and growing a company is something that lasts forever. As a young musician, I worked really hard to save up enough capital to found my first company. Everything I had went into it, and the success of the company showed me that I was on the right path. This may sound old-fashioned, but I found it very rewarding.

People often fear that with a virtual team, their employees may not work when they cannot regularly see or control them. Thus, they become micromanagers or control freaks. How do keep your employees under control? How do you ensure that everyone is giving their best?

Again, from my point of view everything begins with the selection of the right employees for the right place. You want employees who love the upcoming tasks and are focused on their goals. Having fixed appointments to discuss the team's progress greatly helps. The consistent and thorough documentation of what has been discussed and the clear scheduling of objectives and tasks ensures that everyone knows what they have to accomplish. Above all, I signal that the cause and the people involved are important to me. I believe that the problem of control is largely defused if I really transfer competence and responsibility to all participants. But as I said, it needs the right staff.

If I have these things, the next most important thing is the attitude of everyone involved. On the whole, it does not matter to me how many hours an external employee works. From my point of view what matters is that they get the task done. I don't care about effort; I care about results! Look, in the end, the most important thing is that everyone is focused on the goal. In the best-case scenario, everyone gets his recognition through helping the team accomplish its goals. When this is the case, you don't need to control people.

I should say that having fixed dates to meet and confer is in its own way a control function. But because everyone is self-motivated, it doesn't feel like control.

How did you ensure that employees actually get involved in virtual teams and the team is more than the sum of its parts?

The answer to the first part of the question I have already given to the previous question. A team can only achieve more through communication than through the sum of individual skills. It is only when employees exchange ideas that the individual is inspired to be creative. Even in virtual teams, the direct communication is the salt in the soup, which makes a team of top experts a team that is far better than the sum of its individual team members.

Where do you see the future of virtual teams or teams without borders?

Virtual teams are going to become a matter of course, even in areas where they are not found today. With virtual teams, we will be able to overcome the shortage of qualified employees. The world is becoming more and more complex, and the need for specialists in every area is growing. Because of this, companies need to be more flexible than ever before. The classical model of employing hundreds of workers in one geographical location is dying out, and virtual teams are the best solution to give companies this flexibility.

Chapter 11

Extraordinary Achievements
Deserve Extraordinary Rewards – for Everyone

Bernd began to sweat. The thermometer in the gym sauna showed
90 ° C. After an extensive round on the equipment and 2 km on the
treadmill, he enjoyed relaxing. He lay on his towel, his eyes closed, and
felt his body begin to heat up. In that moment, he had to think of the
winter in Transmontania and of the people who should be warm and dry
inside when it is cold outside.

In the latest construction site photos Anne had sent him by email,
the mountain peaks on the horizon were already white. The sight of
the shells of unfinished buildings with snow in the background worried
Bernd. The winter was getting closer, and they had to be faster. Fortunately, the conflict with the head of the Asian construction company had
been taken care of, and everything was back on schedule. But the time
was short. By the middle of December, everything had to be finished,
otherwise the winter would take over.

In some of the photographs,
there were women and even children who helped the construction
workers by carrying ready-made
parts or even buckets of water. In
other pictures, there were villag-
ers standing around the construc-

*The houses in Transmontania
must be finished by the winter.
Bernd is still not sure if they
will succeed, but the team is
ready for the final race.*

tion sites and amazed at what was going on. Suddenly it hissed loudly

- someone had pressed the infusion button. Bernd opened his eyes. The pictures from Transmontania disappeared, and he was back in the sauna in his gym in Hamburg.

A video conference with the extended team was set for the next morning. They would look at the complete project status and the current state of all the team members' goals. Bernd was looking forward to it. He already knew that the members of his core team were on their way to achieving all the goals. The people from the extended team, like Edwin or the other professors from the MOOC, also gave gas and solved many problems independently. The most important suppliers were now familiar with all processes and were constantly kept up to date on the project progress. Bernd could be satisfied. Everything was moving in the right direction. If only winter were not coming so quickly!

The next day, Bernd decided to work from home. In the past months, he had changed a lot. For his German projects, Bernd was now more and more involved by telephone and video conference. Their suppliers and partners had become accustomed to Skype and WebEx. There were still live, personal meetings. But these went more into the depth than before, so that they subsequently regulated much more over the Internet. Even with his German projects, Bernd had made an astounding observation: since he had been showing more interest in his German employees' and partners' personal lives and interests, they have been answering his emails much more quickly and also calling him back more reliably. It was an uphill spiral. The better Bernd knew them, the less friction there was and the more time was spent on fun and personal things on the sidelines. And through these shared positive experiences, you got to know each other even better.

Through this project, Bernd has changed his leadership style. Even with projects in Germany, he works more from home and does more video conferences, and his partners acknowledge that he seems even more interested in them than before.

Whenever Bernd had to carry out strategic or creative tasks, he preferred to do so from home. He enjoyed the convenience and was happy about the extra time he would otherwise have spent in the car. On most days when he worked from the home office, he offered to cook dinner in the evening. Today was one of those days. Wiebke offered to go to the fresh market during her lunch break to get what they needed. He was already looking forward to their dinner together.

Bernd started WebEx as scheduled at 11:00 a.m. All members of the extended team were already logged in. Some said brief hellos, others wrote a greeting in the chat and added a smiling emoticon.

"We are now in the final phase of our project," Bernd began. "Very soon, we will be able to celebrate finishing the first houses and begin the interior decoration. At this point, my very big thanks to Anne, Edwin, Claude, Pilar and their teams, including all suppliers and professors in New York. Together they have managed to speed up the construction work. It is also thanks to them that our relationship with the largest local construction company is again is back on track. Moreover, the relationship has grown more deeply and become more resilient. Now we have to concentrate all our forces once again for the final pace. It is now early November, and we only have six weeks to complete the project."

Claude learns about the competition for an architectural prize. In order to participate in the competition, the team would have to finish two weeks earlier. An enormous challenge.

"Hello again, everyone, and excuse me for interrupting you, Bernd," Claude said. "Are you aware that the International Architecture Summit in Stockholm will take place on December 20th? There are two main prizes to win, one for innovative architecture and another for social responsibility. The closing date for the contest entries is November 30th. And do you know something amusing? All the nominees will be on a large video screen during the conference - live from where they have built their projects, of course. I have already looked at projects on the website from Brazil, Mexico, and the Philippines. Some are similar to what we are doing, but the projects are also more commercial and none of them has to do with helping people in distress. Do you think we should apply?"

"Why not?" Said Bernd. "You know me, Claude. You know I love to win. If this is the one with the greatest social responsibility, that's even better. "

"Unfortunately, there is a catch," Claude explained. "The projects must already have come to an end before the contract is submitted. This is important for the jury to know the exact budget, the time required, and the scope of the project. They also attach importance to a first feedback from the builders, or in the case of more socially-oriented projects, the residents. We would have to hurry and finish two weeks earlier if we want to participate in the competition."

"That would be a miracle," moaned Bernd. "Anne, Edwin, Linda, Pilar what do you think?"

They voted. They would have to spur the construction workers and the local population once more, was the unanimous opinion.

"It just so happens that December 20th is a religious holiday," Anne said with her calm voice. "Perhaps it might be an incentive to tell people the following: If everything is finished by November 30th, and you help us and try really hard to finish early, then you will have time to move into your new homes and set everything up in peace, so that you will be able to celebrate on December 20th together with your Family in your new house. I can well imagine that the construction workers would be glad to give more overtime for this goal."

"Anne, in your photos I see a lot of people who help the construction workers," Bernd said. "There seems to be a strong sense of togetherness in Transmontania. How would it be if we were to organize the already available help a bit better? For example, we could recruit whole groups of volunteers who commit themselves to do a certain number of hours of work. The construction workers can assist the volunteers and give them clear instructions on what to do. Not in a typical German manner, but if everything had an orderly framework, these volunteers could contribute a lot more."

In order to be able to cope more quickly, the team decides to involve more local residents. Volunteers help with the project so that families can celebrate an upcoming holiday in their new homes.

"I will contact the mayors and the religious leaders," Anne replied. "The population is very enthusiastic about the matter, we can count on that. But we need the support of the local authorities. Also, I'm not sure if the construction workers alone will be able to get the people involved. We may need a few coaches and organizers with specialized organizational skills."

"We have students from Transmontania in our MOOC!" Edwin cried. "I guess that's about 25 people. Let me make contact with them, and I can see if I can activate them. I would be thrilled not only work on the blueprints alone but to be able to help with the practical execution."

"Great idea, Edwin!" said Bernd. "On the one hand, we need experts who are familiar with the new buildings and the special construction method, and this is only possible if we know our blueprints. On the other hand, we need people who speak the language of the people in Transmontania. The students would be ideal for this!"

"Edwin, could you physically be here during the intense phase?" Anne asked cautiously. "I know you are in China and, well, Transmontania is not exactly around the corner, but it would be great if you could be here on the ground. "

"I will definitely stay there long enough to find enough volunteers and to hold a workshop with the students, so that they know what we expect them to do. We should probably first develop a plan of how best to involve the volunteers, how to train them, how to distribute their duties, and to determine who will be managing their whole involvement. Once our team has established which duties the volunteers will have, I will have to fly back to China for a week, but I'll remain in close contact with the project from there."

"Thank you very much," Anne said tightly, in her usual sober and reserved manner. "We can communicate the details as soon as you have arrived here."

"Hey, I have an idea!" That was Stella. "So far, we have made quite conventional status reports - bar charts, pie diagrams, and explanatory texts. Why do not we visualize project progress much more? There are some interesting, new trends. You can show the status of the project on a slide with a picture so that everyone can see with a glance where we stand. It could, for example, be a tree and hang on the tree fruits in the traditional colors of all places in Transmontania where we have building sites. The size of the fruit indicates the percentage of the houses completed in each location. I was once in a project where they worked with such a visualization, and it worked out very well. For weeks, people kept looking at the site to see how we were progressing. It is really motivating to see how a project is progressing. If you all agree, I will create a slide for it. "

With the help of local MOOC students, Edwin wants to recruit volunteers. Stella also has a novel idea for a more motivating form of the status report.

"I like your idea," Linda said. "If you like, I'll send you some suggestions within the next two days."

Stella agreed. And Bernd felt great. He was proud of his team. At the same time, he felt humbled by how engaged and thoughtful his was. He knew his team had done a great job over the last few weeks. It had organized itself and mastered all the challenges. He himself had contributed very little to it. But that did not matter, because he had given his team members the authority they needed to act independently and with passion.

"Let us go with this," said Bernd. "We are a great team, and I have no doubt that we can finish the houses by the end of November. If we win one of the two main prizes in Stockholm - or even the shortlist - then that will be a top reference for us all, and we may get a lot of new assignments. In addition, perhaps even more of our budget will remain intact if we finish two weeks earlier. Then we can use this money to bring everyone to Transmontania so we can celebrate together on December 20th. After all the problems that we have already mastered, it is now an enormous challenge to finish two weeks earlier. But with the passion you have shown up until now and with the enthusiasm of local people for their homes and the religious festival, I am firmly convinced that we can do it!"

There are more Effective Rewards than Money or the Usual Bonuses

Several times in this book I have dealt with the importance of recognition and a functioning reward system for virtual teams. Every team member needs genuine and honest recognition. Lack of recognition is one of the main reasons people leave a team. At this point, however, I am not asking for recognition in general but for exceptional team performance. Such a special prize should never simply be money or some other conventional bonus, such as stock options. The reward should be a highly emotional experience for the entire team. It has to be an event that every single team member is looking forward to. Because the members of virtual teams rarely see each other personally, a community event is often a very good reward for everyone.

A special prize, which is to motivate the team to top performances, must also be something very special. Money is not enough. It should be a unique experience for everyone!

Acknowledgments

The use of selections from copyrighted material has been graciously granted by the following publishers and copyright holders.

"The Deming Way" by Mike Schmoker. Copyright © 1992. Used by permission of the author.

The Effective Executive by Peter F. Drucker. Copyright © 1966, 1967 by Peter F. Drucker. HarperCollins Publishers Inc. Used by permission.

Reprinted by permission of Warner Books/New York from *If It Ain't Broke . . . BREAK IT!* Copyright 1991 by Robert J. Kriegel.

It Doesn't Take a Hero by General H. Norman Schwarzkopf and Peter Petre. Copyright © 1992 by H. Norman Schwarzkopf. Used by permission of Bantam Books, a division of Bantam Doubleday Dell Publishing Group, Inc.

The Leadership Challenge by James M. Kouzes and Barry Z. Posner. Copyright © 1987. Jossey-Bass Publishers. Reprinted by permission of the publisher. World rights in the English language only.

Leadership Is an Art by Max DePree. Copyright © 1967 by Max DePree. Used by permission of Doubleday, a division of Bantam Doubleday Dell Publishing Group, Inc.

Leadership Jazz by Max DePree. Copyright © 1992 by Doubleday, a division of Bantam Doubleday Dell Publishing Group, Inc.

Life's Little Instruction Book by H. Jackson Brown, Jr. Copyright © 1991. Rutledge Hill Press. Reprinted by permission of the publisher.

Management Decisions by Objectives by George S. Odiorne. Copyright © 1969. Used by permission of Prentice Hall/Career and Personal Development.

Managing for the Future by Peter Drucker. Copyright © 1992 by Peter Drucker. A Truman Talley Book. Used by permission of Dutton Signet, a division of Penguin Books USA Inc.

Preparing Instructional Objectives by Robert F. Mager. Copyright © 1984. Lake Publishing Co. Reprinted by permission of the publisher.

Reprinted with permission of the publisher from *The Time Trap: New Version of the Classic Book on Time Management* © 1972 Alec Mackenzie. Published by AMACOM, a Division of the American Management Association. All rights reserved.

War As I Knew It by George S. Patton. Copyright 1947 by Beatrice Patton Waters, Ruth Patton Totten and George Smith Patton. Copyright © renewed 1975 by Major General George Patton, Ruth Patton Totten, John K. Waters, Jr., George P. Waters. Reprinted by permission of Houghton Mifflin Company. All rights reserved.

"Wanted, Executive Time Power" by Frank A. Nunlist (1967). Used by permission.

"Where Do You Stand?" by William G. Saltonstall (1961). Used by permission.

Every effort has been made to find copyright holders. For those whom we have not included, both the publisher and the author will be pleased to make the necessary arrangements at the first opportunity.

① Leadership—The Person

We begin with the assumption that you are already a leader in church activities or that you will be, which leads us to a second assumption: because the Lord's work is involved, you want to do the best possible job as a leader. A third assumption leads us to conclude that you have had life experiences that form a foundation for your leadership. Experience has already convinced you of the need for some of the leadership qualities we will discuss. You may believe that particular qualities are obvious, but as we will see in our case histories, many church leaders fail because they have not incorporated these specific qualities into their leadership style.

What Is Leadership?

Leadership has been called the most important management challenge today. Business and administrative schools continue to conduct research in order to teach men and women how to become effective leaders. Such knowledge is important for anyone involved in a leadership role in service of the Church.

Leadership is not custodial care of a lifeless organization. Leadership involves actively and creatively presiding over a *living* organization in an ever-changing environment. The manner in which one presides is extremely important.

What, then, is this mysterious thing called leadership that allows some people to effectively unite the efforts of others in accomplishing goals while many would-be leaders fail? Leadership is the art of influencing the actions of others in such a way as to gain their respect, confidence, and loyal, wholehearted cooperation in accomplishing an established goal. Leadership calls for special qualities in those who want to be effective leaders.

Sound leadership motivates subordinates, employees, or volunteers to perform well. It encourages them to use their talents and initiative and to develop their potential to attain their organization's goals. It is flexible. It meets changing organizational needs.

Drivership, on the other hand, is controlling and rigid. It strangles initiative. It is stagnating. It smothers the creativity of subordinates, employees, and volunteers alike. It limits their performance and growth.

Which of these two styles—leadership or drivership—work the best? In *Leadership Is an Art,* Max DePree describes the art of leadership as ". . . liberating people to do what is required of them in the most effective and humane way possible."[1]

Consider these case studies:

- Pastor A is bewildered by his continually declining church attendance in spite of his extensive efforts to be in charge of all major and minor activities. His volunteers eventually quit. His salaried help frequently leave when they are able to find other employment. Because they know how hard the pastor works, no one can find the words to tell him of the underlying cause of their dissatisfaction.

- Pastor B is in a neighboring parish. His congregation is growing. People often comment on the team spirit that permeates the parish's various activities. They especially like the excellent music that is offered and cannot help but comment on how much the music minister obviously enjoys her work. The pastor recognizes the talents of both salaried staff and volunteers and is careful to encourage their initiative and personal growth. People enjoy working for him.

Pastor B has the ability to liberate people for effective performance. Pastor A lacks that skill. Ultimately, the people in the congregation pay the price!

The newly arrived leader in any organization inherits an authority that keeps the organization operating. But employees and volunteers soon will be evaluating their new boss. It is a wise leader who realizes that one cannot rely on the temporary deference to authority to produce long-term results.

Research conducted by professors James M. Kouzes and Barry Z. Posner of Santa Clara University caused them to conclude that

> Followers determine whether someone possesses leadership qualities. Upper management cannot confer leadership on someone they select to manage a unit. Over time, those who would be followers will determine whether that person should be—and will be—recognized as a leader. Leadership is in the eye of the follower.[2]

The good news is that effective leadership can be learned. Business and management expert Peter Drucker underscores that point. "Effectiveness . . . is a habit; that is, a complex of practices. And practices can always be learned."[3]

We can begin looking at the complexity of leadership by breaking it into four categories, which we will discuss here and in chapters 2, 3, and 4: the person of the leader, the approach a leader takes to fill that role, rules of the leadership game, and the business of leadership.

The personal qualities or traits that leaders possess will have a definite impact upon those who work for them. They may not be able to identify or name those qualities, but they are decidedly influenced by them. Let's take a look at the qualities that are the hallmarks of an effective leader, remembering that they can be developed or improved by anyone who wants to enhance leadership performance.

The Traits of an Effective Leader

Appearance—A Matter of Image

The image a leader projects is perhaps the most important quality on our list. A positive image is the combination of a number of factors that help create a favorable impression. You have no doubt noticed the effort made by people running for public office to establish a positive image. Positive image is a combination of personal appearance, bearing, and conduct.

Clergy cannot neglect their image any more than can the president of a large corporation—that is, if they want to be successful. People who work for the Church may not have the finest clothes, but their clothes should fit well, be clean, and be in good repair. Personal cleanliness and neatness is a must. Good grooming is a significant factor in forming your image. In a busy world of parish life there may be a temptation to allow one's appearance to slide. Check yourself out in a mirror. Taking the time to have a favorable appearance is a requirement for the professional side of a leader's image.

The way you walk, stand, sit, and move can project an image of either confidence or a feeling of inferiority. Consider this simple advice on projecting a favorable image taken from *Life's Little Instruction Book* by H. Jackson Brown, Jr.: "Have good posture. Enter a room with purpose and confidence."[4]

Your behavior—on and off "duty"—will tell others much about their leader's character. Your demeanor does make a difference.

A favorable image is equally important for other leaders within the church organization—the director of religious education, the music minister, and committee heads, for example. Everyone in a position of leadership needs to project a positive image.

In summary, your image tells others what they may expect of you. It makes a statement about how you feel about yourself and your work. Your image, then, calls for careful analysis and a willingness to make improvements, if necessary.

Courage

Leaders in some lines of work clearly need to display the trait of courage. Commanders of fire, police, and military units, for example, must be willing to endure the same dangers as those whom they direct.

- Sergeant Ed Freeman commanded a police SWAT unit whose mission was to enter a building and arrest a man who had been firing a rifle at people in the street. The only way that Sergeant

Freeman could lead was by entering the building with his team. It was part of the job and was expected of an effective team leader.

There are times when a minister, rabbi, or priest will find themselves in a dangerous situation as well. Risks taken by military chaplains in battle are mirrored by other clergy who may be forced to confront an emotionally disturbed individual, a dangerous criminal, or a violent person. One's faith in God is a powerful resource in such cases.

But courage is called for in many less dramatic instances. You may have to correct a misguided volunteer. You may have to terminate an employee for misconduct or poor performance. Facing such unpleasant tasks calls for courage to meet one of the obligations of leadership.

- Pastor P. P. was a caring and sensitive man in charge of a large, active parish and school as well as a historic church and church grounds that were quite popular with visitors and tour groups. He used an accounting firm in another city because the firm's bookkeeper was the daughter of a former long-time employee. Although she was only a contracted bookkeeper, she functioned as an absentee business manager, approving or disapproving purchase requests and establishing her own financial policies and procedures. The operational and financial needs of parish, school, and historical site had to await her weekly visits. Frequent payroll errors were not corrected, and bills were often not paid on time. Employees complained that their requests for needed supplies were turned down or the quantities were arbitrarily reduced. It was painful for the pastor to end the services of the firm, which, of course, also meant the termination of the personal relationship as well. Finally, with increased pressure from the staff and the finance committee, he did what had to be done and established an efficient finance and purchasing operation "in house." The termination was very difficult for the pastor, but one that was clearly necessary.

In summary, to be an effective leader, you will need to have the courage to face unpleasant tasks and take appropriate action. It goes with the job!

Decisiveness

Decisiveness is the ability to make sound decisions promptly and then state them in a clear and concise manner. The decisive quality in leadership arises from your vision, anticipation of future events, and well thought-out goals. (The development of goals will be discussed in chapter 6.)

When you have clear vision of where your enterprise is headed in the future, many of your decisions can be made easily. It is the poor leader who has given little or no thought to the future who finds him- or herself unprepared and often caught up in someone else's agenda.

Naturally not all future events can be anticipated, and some decisions may have to be delayed until you have an opportunity to study possible solutions. You can minimize the number of such surprises, however, by your vision of the future.

The need for decisions will arise in minor as well as major matters. Your incoming mail, for example, will involve many minor decisions. Are you a compulsive reader?

- As a consequence of his many years in the ministry, Reverend J. E. was on numerous mailing lists. He discovered that more than 90 percent of his mail was unsolicited material. Reading each piece of mail could consume a significant amount of time each day. After quickly checking the return address to see if it might be an item of interest, he began discarding mail that did not have first-class postage. The time saved was used much more productively.

- Mrs. P. M. was hired as a secretary for a large parish. She discovered that the pastor, who had been processing his own mail, had boxes of unopened letters dating back three years. The letters contained donations, prayer requests, and other matters never acted upon. The decision-making process had become too burdensome, so it had been deferred!

- Mr. M. B., a business executive in a large corporation, advises making decisions promptly on most matters involving the daily mail. "There is a temptation to put off decisions on some minor matters 'until later,'" he said, "but the end result is a deep stack of paper which is not acted upon. Taking an extra moment or two to add a note and route the item to someone for action can improve your effectiveness."

Decisiveness does not involve making snap decisions. It involves making decisions that are based upon established vision, philosophy, and goals.

To help you work your way through difficult decisions, a decision-making process is discussed in chapter 2 in the section "Make Sound and Timely Decisions."

In summary, you will find that most decisions can be made with very little effort when you draw upon your vision, general philosophy, and goals. Unexpected developments can usually be put on hold while you complete the problem-solving process. While this process can lead to appropriate actions, some decisions will still be difficult to make. Even when decisions are tough, sound decisions will gain the respect of those you lead.

Dependability

For a leader dependability means the certainty of the proper and timely performance of one's work. As a leader you will be expected to do your best work, both by your superior and by your subordinates.

The quality of dependability is also furthered by a leader's vision, goals, and philosophy. Decisions are made that are consistent with past decisions, and this reliability strengthens the leader's relationship with those who follow.

Dependability builds a climate of trust that is so essential for good leadership. In the words of professors Kouzes and Posner, ". . . do what you say you are going to do. That may be as simple as getting to a meeting on time. It may be as difficult as not firing anyone during a downturn if you have declared you have a no-layoff policy."[5]

Some leaders fail in the dependability department because they are unwilling to limit their activities. They believe they must accommodate everyone. As a result, their performance is unpredictable. Here's an example of what can happen:

- Pastor M. P. was a kindly man who was reluctant to say "no" to almost any request. He often made verbal commitments without checking his calendar. He frequently committed himself to be in two or more places at the same time, causing delays and missed appointments. It also caused others in the organization frequently to drop their activities to fill in for him at a moment's notice.

In summary, effective leaders are dependable and consistent. You will want a good record of reliability. Those who follow you will know what to expect.

Enthusiasm

Enthusiasm is the display of sincere interest in the performance of one's work. The leader who does not enjoy his or her work will have difficulty in inspiring others to perform well. Enthusiasm is contagious!

The enthusiastic leader is one who constantly seeks new information about his or her field. After all, the Christian religion did not stop growing in self-understanding two thousand years ago. Subscriptions to quality religious journals and periodicals, for example, can build enthusiasm in a field that continues to discover new historical data and gain new insights into the inexhaustible riches of the faith.

How important is enthusiasm in influencing others?

- Dr. James Covert is a dynamic history professor at the University of Portland in Oregon. Each semester at registration time his classes fill up quickly. His reputation as a superb instructor is well known. Dr. Covert states that he became a history professor because as a child he listened to interesting discussions of history at his family's dinner table. He later discovered that many history teachers made the subject boring. Students were turned off. He resolved that he would teach history in a way that would make it come alive for his students. His natural talent was given a great boost by his enthusiasm.

Charles Schwab, a successful steel executive in the early 1920s, credited his ability to arouse enthusiasm among his employees to be his greatest asset.[6]

Professors Kouzes and Posner observe, ". . . it is essential that leaders inspire our confidence in the validity of the goal. Enthusiasm and excitement signal the leader's personal commitment to pursuing that dream. If a leader displays no passion for a cause, why should others?"[7]

In summary, you will succeed in inspiring top performance in others when you show your own enthusiasm.

Initiative

Initiative is the quality of seeing what needs to be done and then doing it.

A leader who waits to be told what is to be done either lacks initiative or has a boss who insists on making all of the decisions. Leaders who destroy the creativity of their staff deprive them of job satisfaction and seriously damage their own organization.

The competent leader not only uses initiative but also encourages others to do so. "The effect of enabling others to act is to make them feel strong, capable and committed," declare Kouzes and Posner. "Those in the organization who must produce the results feel a sense of ownership. They feel empowered, and when people feel empowered, they are more likely to use their energies to produce extraordinary results."[8]

- Officer Don Hochstein was assigned as a training instructor in a metropolitan police department. He was a highly creative teacher who frequently approached his supervisors with plans for new and improved training methods. His superiors recognized his talent and approved his plans. As a result, the entire agency benefited. He enthusiastically continued to use his initiative to devise new training programs for his department.

- Mr. C. D. was a part-time computer operator for a large parish in a busy community. When the pastor reorganized the business office and dropped an outside accounting firm, he placed C. D. in charge of all data processing. He was able to establish a number of cost-effective programs that were far better and less costly than those provided by the accounting firm.

In summary, as an effective leader, you should not only use initiative to accomplish your own work, you should also encourage capable subordinates to use their initiative. People who actively participate in their organization tend to enjoy their work more.

Integrity

Integrity is strength of character and soundness of moral principle, but it also includes the ability to be truthful and honest. The quality of integrity is essential for a leader, for it builds trust. When dishonesty, untruthfulness, or other forms of immoral behavior are attributed to a leader, the results are disastrous. As we have seen in our own time, the news media quickly sensationalize detected weaknesses in public figures. Church personalities are certainly not exempt.

Not only must the life of the leader be free of such defects; one must also take a clear and aggressive stand to promote virtues within the organization. Tremendous damage can be done in an organization by a leader who fails to take prompt and appropriate action against the immoral as well as the incompetent.

• The business manager of a large church activity was accused of sexual harassment by a female employee. Although the complaint was promptly investigated and verified by a member of the staff, the pastor delayed in taking appropriate disciplinary action. As a result, the employee retained an attorney and filed a law suit. The news media publicized the complaint, and the incident gained unnecessary and unfortunate notoriety.

There is a tendency in church circles to hope that embarrassing incidents will fade away. Some even hope that the responsible authority, by not taking action against the offending party, will be seen as a person of peace and understanding. As an effective leader, you cannot permit such compromise of standards.

Some years ago William G. Saltonstall, principal of Phillips Exeter Academy, made the following commentary in *This Week Magazine:*

Certainly many of us agree that the exercise of restraint is one of the marks of the good man. But in some areas compromise is flabby and dangerous. Any person of real conviction and strength must choose one side of the road or the other. It would be a strange kind of education that urged us to be "relatively" honest, "sometimes" just, "usually" tolerant, "for the most part" decent.⁹

In summary, as a leader, you must be a person whose personal conduct, behavior, and truthfulness are exemplary. You must also be recognized as one who will not condone inappropriate, immoral, or dishonest behavior by those for whom you are responsible.

Judgment

Judgment is the process of making sound decisions. Judgment involves weighing facts and possible solutions to arrive at a well thought-out course of action.

When a leader has the reputation of frequently making poor decisions, it is usually because of a failure to carefully gather facts and analyze their bearing on possible consequences. In other words, poor decisions are often the result of a failure to "look down the road" and visualize what would happen if each option were acted upon.

- Bishop M. N. often made decisions based on emotion, or what others called his "gut reaction." It was a good example of a failure to "look down the road." His decisions, often made in haste, were also at times explosive. He found it difficult to understand why his actions produced negative consequences. His failures were particularly evident in personnel matters and personal relations.

- Pastor M. P. learned from experience that his decisions often met with objections from other members of the staff who pointed out the likely unfavorable consequences. This troubled him, for he was eager to assert that he was in charge of the parish. As a result, he chose not to discuss any pending decisions. He became quiet and secretive before making major decisions. His staff was unable to help him.

Gathering opposing ideas can help you make better decisions. Management expert Peter Drucker advises, "The understanding that underlies the right decision grows out of the clash and conflict of divergent opinions and out of the serious consideration of competing alternatives."[10]

No one has a perfect record, but the leader who discovers that personal decisions are often faulty should follow the process recommended in "Making Sound and Timely Decisions" in chapter 2. If followed and poor decisions are still made, it is a signal for the leader to learn to consult with advisers. They may be staff members or experts in appropriate fields. If they offer divergent views, so much the better. In fact, truly effective leaders seek the participation of others in making decisions.

Many giants of business and industry have credited their success to their ability to gather around themselves people who were more capable than they were. Millionaire Andrew Carnegie credited those who helped build his success. The epitaph he prepared for his tombstone read, "Here lies one who knew how to get around him men who were cleverer than himself."[11]

You can use this same principle in selecting a staff, assistants, or helpers. Be on the lookout for creative people with a vision of the future. Then give them the freedom to use their talents.

In summary, as a leader, your record for making sound decisions will determine if others believe that your judgment can be trusted. Having good judgment is a significant aspect of your professional reputation that can be strengthened by your ability to enlist quality people to work on your team.

Knowledge

Two vastly different areas of knowledge are important for the leader: acquired knowledge (which includes one's professional background) and knowledge of the people one supervises.

Leaders usually are selected for their positions by proving they have acquired the knowledge necessary to perform their job well. But we live in an age in which new information emerges at an incredible rate. Professional people in our society find it necessary to attend workshops, lectures, seminars, and do professional reading to keep up on developments in their field. It is equally true of church professions that one can no longer run on yesterday's knowledge.

Because of the dramatic increase of knowledge in many professions, specialization has become essential. The church leader today may be either a specialist or a generalist, but there is an ever-present challenge to grow professionally.

The computer age gives ministry an effective tool that can be used for increased efficiency. Many leaders within the Church need to at least become familiar with what computers can do in the hands of a trained operator.

Developments in medicine bring new moral issues to be pondered, while Scripture studies in recent years give new insights on God's saving presence in the world. New concepts in liturgy, liturgical art, and music have emerged, making worship more relevant for people. Consequently, the church leader should be well-educated and stay in touch with current developments within and outside the Church.

Continuing education is not a luxury—it is essential for today's leader. You will need to make time in a busy schedule to allow for professional growth.

- Reverend J. C. was an associate pastor in a busy parish, but he made time to pursue his interests in computer science and music at a nearby community college. Not only did these courses broaden his background but also his interaction with younger students was intellectually stimulating. It provided an opportunity for students to discover that a clergyman is a genuine human being as well!

Apart from the acquired knowledge that is crucial to one's job performance, the leader needs to know the people in his or her working environment. The leader needs to know and care about them.

Certainly the church leader should be sensitive to those workers who are having severe difficulties in their lives. Family problems, illness, an unemployed spouse, or the loss of a loved one can affect one's concentration, level of energy, and overall performance. Knowing the burden a worker is carrying will help you deal with that person more effectively.

Knowing those who work for you also means knowing their strengths and weaknesses. It enables you to use their gifts more appropriately and more creatively. It enables you to assign the right task to the right person.

The opportunity to have contact with those who do the work is considered so important in some corporations that executives take special measures to be among them. It is an opportunity for communication. It is getting to know those who are closest to what we do.

Management experts remind us that ". . . sensitivity to others is a prerequisite for success in leadership. . . . So schedule some time daily just to get acquainted with [them]."[12]

- Mr. D. R. is the music minister in an active parish. Although the choir is large, he greets each person by name as they arrive for evening practice. He makes a special inquiry about members of the family and how they are getting along. Members enjoy being in his choir because his sensitive attitude is contagious, and they find themselves as part of a caring community.

You can demonstrate your knowledge of and caring about those working for you in many ways. A card to each person on his or her birthday assures them that they are remembered and important to you. Enter their birthdays on your appointment calendar. A wise boss will also remember Secretaries' Day each April.

In summary, as a modern leader you cannot rely only upon knowledge gained in the past. The role of leadership requires that the search for knowledge and truth continues as a lifelong effort. You will also want to know the people you lead and the small and large events that are important to them. Knowledge gives you the power to lead more effectively.

Loyalty

For the church leader, loyalty means faithfulness to God, to one's denomination, superior, religious community, congregation, country, local community, and subordinates. The need for loyalty in any enterprise is essential for its success. Consequently, it is an essential quality for the leader.

What may be surprising is the concept that a leader needs to be loyal to those who are followers. A leader should have genuine and continuing interest in their well-being. A leader should not only give moral support when they encounter difficulties but also have an active concern about their working and living conditions.

All too often it is the church worker who is poorly paid, has few, if any, fringe benefits, and is expected to work on holidays. It is ironic that some church officials who advocate "just wages for workers" pay their own employees so poorly. Their attention is focused upon someone else's turf. They are unaware of the hardships endured by their own staff.

- Mr. R. C. is the church sacristan and also functions as the plant maintenance worker. Because of his duties as sacristan he is expected to be on hand at all major and most minor church functions. As a maintenance man, he is also expected to work "normal" working hours. Consequently, on religious holidays he spends most of the day away from his family. He receives no compensatory time off—his daily presence is too important! He is often called in on days off and vacation days when a maintenance problem materializes at the church or school. His salary is well below that of others in the community who have similar duties and responsibilities.

- Mr. J. S. was hired as the business manager (or, as he preferred to say, "Chief Operations Officer" [C.O.O.]) of a large church activity. Eager to solidify his position with the pastor (whom he liked to call the "Chief Executive Officer" [C.E.O.]), J. S. recommended changing health plans to save money. The pastor agreed. The change meant that employees lost health insurance coverage for family members. In order to include a spouse and child under the new plan, an employee would need to have an extra $200 deducted from monthly take-home pay. In businesses where employees are represented by unions, such a change in benefits would result in a formal grievance.

No one was there to take the side of the employees at this church, however.

As a church leader, you will need to protect the benefits and working conditions of those for whom you are responsible. Loyalty toward the workers must not be forgotten.

Loyalty toward one's superiors means that you will support the goals and tasks you are given. If you disagree with the boss' policy, it would be appropriate to say so in a private discussion. But loyalty requires that disagreements not be discussed publicly.

In summary, as a leader your loyalty is required not only toward your supervisor but also for those whom you supervise.

Tact

Tact is the ability to deal with others without creating offense. It is a particularly vital quality for a leader. The importance of dealing tactfully with your boss may be obvious, but it is no less important in dealing with subordinates.

Leadership that "works," you will recall, is based upon gaining followers' loyal, wholehearted cooperation. So you can see how important it is to treat the follower—both employee and volunteer—with a large helping of respect. Tact is the lubricant that keeps human relations running smoothly.

Dale Carnegie's timeless work *How to Win Friends and Influence People* is an excellent book on human relations that has been a best-seller for decades. It should be read and reread by anyone who is serious about refining leadership skills. Carnegie emphasizes the importance of tact in dealing with others.[13]

- Bishop Y. M. is accustomed to receiving deference from others because of his position and title. Memos written to his clergy often include hostile words. Conferences, too, are salted with angry messages. One priest reported to his colleagues that the bishop "became livid" when he discussed a new compensation schedule for diocesan clergy. Unfortunately, the poor bishop is unaware that his lack of tact has an extremely negative effect upon his clergy.

The way in which a leader presents his or her observations is every bit as important as the actual words. Consider the following example of a tactful method of making corrections:

- Reverend E. S. is a chaplain in a city police department. Two employees work for him: a police officer and a secretary. At times it is necessary for him to correct their performance. E. S. likes to use the "sandwich technique." This technique involves recognizing specific instances of good performance of the employee before and after offering the correction. He tactfully "sandwiches" his suggested improvement between two positive "slices" of praise. The conference always ends on a positive note, and the employee looks forward to making the recommended improvement.

The language and the manner with which corrections are made are important elements of tact. The time and place for making corrections are also important. Whenever possible, corrections should be a private matter. "A leader ought never to embarrass followers," says business executive Max DePree.[14]

In summary, as a leader, tact will help your interpersonal relations to function smoothly. You will want to be as tactful in dealing with your employees and volunteers as you are with you boss. The "sandwich technique" is a useful tool for improving others' performance in a constructive, energizing way.

Unselfishness

For a leader, unselfishness means the avoidance of providing for one's own comfort and personal advancement at the expense of others. Father John Powell, the well-known Jesuit educator and author, states that when the happiness, security, and well-being of another means more to us than our own needs, we can truly say that we love that person.[15] Love entails a complete abandonment of selfishness.

From a leadership perspective, then, unselfishness means putting the happiness, security, and well-being of employees and volunteers ahead of your own self-interest.

Unselfishness is demonstrated by the practice of good military leaders who wait to eat until the last of their troops is fed; that is, assuring that there is enough food for others before taking their own meal.

Unselfishness for the church leader may involve the willingness to put aside one's own work or favorite activity to listen to the troubles of an employee or volunteer. It may mean offering to preside at a church function in order for a colleague to have some time off.

There is something fundamentally Christian about putting the well-being of others ahead of individual interests. Many opportunities arise in surprising circumstances. Effective leadership, though, requires balance. A forced effort to prove you are unselfish can interfere with your essential duties. Pastor M. P., the man who couldn't say "no," fell into this trap and disrupted his own schedule and those of others in the parish.

In summary, as a leader, you should be aware of the necessity of considering the well-being of those who follow you and placing their needs ahead of your own. You should remember their need for affirmation and generously give them credit for helping you accomplish your goals and objectives.

Personal Qualities of Leaders

Appearance–Professional Image
Courage
Decisiveness
Dependability
Enthusiasm
Initiative
Integrity
Judgment
Knowledge
Loyalty
Tact
Unselfishness

Fig. 1. Summary of personal qualities.

② The Approach to Leadership

We have examined the person of a leader, looking at the qualities or traits that bring about effectiveness. We can work to improve any weak areas. Equally important, however, is the manner in which one approaches one's work. Effective leaders are guided in their leadership roles by a series of principles.

Know Your Job

Leaders who fail to grasp the major elements of their job will be unable to gain the respect of their followers. The person newly appointed to a leadership position may experience some uncertainties about a new role. Even an experienced leader who moves into a new position will need a period of adjustment.

Where do you start in order to know what your job entails?

A well-run organization will provide job descriptions for every position. They form the basis for agreement between worker and supervisor. Job descriptions are discussed in greater detail in chapter 8.

You should have a job description provided by the person to whom you are responsible. If no job description exists, you will find it helpful to create one based on your vision of the job. You can use it as the basis for a discussion with the person to whom you report. A bit of diplomacy is called for here. Explain that you want to clearly understand his or her expectations so that you can meet them. A mutually agreed upon job description can prevent needless uncertainty and possible conflict down the road.

- Newly ordained priests in a large diocese were placed in a three-year internship program. They were instructed to meet with their pastors and devise a "contract" that would spell out their expectations. This contract would be reviewed during the year and rewritten for the following years of the program. Such contracts are another form of a job description.

It is obvious that the job description of a director of religious education will be quite different from that of a music minister. What is not so obvious is that the job descriptions for clergy may be quite different, according to their assignments. Ordination does not bring an across-the-board expertise that prepares one for any and all assignments. A general, all-purpose job description will not do.

The demands of your job may change, or you may be reassigned. Either situation may call for new knowledge and skills. The principle of knowing your job can be most challenging.

In summary, as a leader you will be expected to know your job and be proficient in it. A written job description is an important guide in establishing what is expected of you. You will also need to have some understanding of the jobs of those who work for you, even if you lack the special skills to perform those jobs. Be alert for changes that may occur in the job you have been performing.

Know Yourself and Seek Improvement

Each of us brings together a unique combination of strengths and weaknesses. Effective leaders identify their weaknesses, and when possible, seek improvement. We have already noted that in today's rapidly developing world there is a need among professionals for continuing education. It is not just a matter of new information being discovered and new techniques being devised—the demands of your job may change.

- Pastor J. C. found himself in a parish with a changing ethnic composition. He took classes in Spanish at a nearby community college. He eventually attended a language school in Mexico to totally immerse himself in the language. This effort brought a dramatic improvement in his ability to minister to Spanish-speaking parishioners.

• Early in the computer age pastor T. W. saw the advantages of computerizing parish records and programs. He tutored himself in this newly emerging field. His fairly small parish benefited from his personal commitment to professional growth.

• Mr. J. H. is a lay minister interested in expanding his ministry to hospital work. He enrolled in a death and dying course at a local university to enable himself to deal more effectively with the terminally ill and their families.

Physical fitness is an area that most of us need to improve. Fortunately, we live in an age in which public attention has been focused on the necessity for maintaining proper diet and exercise. Unfortunately, those in a busy ministry may neglect them. But a correct diet and sufficient exercise are not luxuries. They are important components of a health maintenance program as are regular physical examinations to detect medical problems early on.

• Reverend T. O. regularly schedules the time to take a walk around his community. In this way not only does he maintain his exercise program he also enjoys healthy interactions with the people he encounters. It is an effective use of time, both physically and socially.

• Reverend H. J. believes that he would preach more effectively without using notes. He was concerned, however, with his poor memory. He worked to make his homilies reasonably brief and organized his main points in a logical sequence. He wrote them down, then prepared an outline of key words on a card to be carried in his pocket as an emergency reference in case of memory failure. As he gained increased confidence he stopped carrying the card. He developed the ability to speak to large congregations in a personal and direct way with excellent results.

In summary, as an effective leader you will want to identify your strengths and weaknesses—then find ways to improve them. It may be a matter of health, interpersonal relations, or some elements of your job performance. But the desire to always improve underlies good leadership.

Know Your Workers
and Look Out for Their Welfare

The president of a large manufacturing corporation will probably not know the names of every employee on the factory floor, but, even so, visits to the work area undoubtedly will make an impression. It will prove that their boss cares about them. The major general who commands an infantry division will not know the names of the troops in the mess hall, but they will be aware that "the old man" cares enough about them to eat the same food they have—and evaluate it.

While top leaders cannot know the names of all persons at the working level, certainly their immediate supervisor should. In the same way, the music minister of a parish should know the names and something about the people in the choir.

Knowing the employees and volunteers along with their strengths and weaknesses will enable you to appropriately assign them to new tasks and consider them for positions of increased responsibility. Unions play a key role in improving the working conditions of their members and assuring fair play. In the Church, however, employees and volunteers are usually not represented by any articulate, influential outside party. Consequently, the need for attention to workers' welfare clearly falls upon the leader.

- Recall our earlier case of Mr. J. S., the C.O.O. for a large church activity who arranged for a new health plan to save money. Consequently, employees lost health coverage for their family members. Without formal representation to protest actions that damage employees' working conditions and benefits, workers may be placed in a vulnerable position. Thus, the pastor must be deeply committed and sensitive to their needs.

- Bishop N. N. sent a lengthy memo to his clergy, promising them a salary increase in six months. He admitted that an increase was three years overdue. He concluded his memo by railing against using the consumer price index as a means of establishing the increased cost of living. His clergy noted that not only did they have to wait for an increase that was three years overdue, they would have to wait an additional six months to gain any salary increase. The bishop had no idea of the hard feelings his "generosity" engendered and the continued decline in the morale of his clergy.

A pastor who has associates living in the same rectory has a special obligation to consider their welfare and comfort. The old saying that the rectory is the pastor's house and that others are merely guests recognizes a rather informal perquisite seized upon by pastors. But make no mistake about it; it is contrary to the principles of good leadership. The leader is responsible for the well-being of those in subordinate positions.

• Reverend R. W. was the second associate pastor assigned to a parish church. He discovered that the pastor had two dogs that were not housebroken. They had the run of the rectory, which created a foul odor. The house cook was an indifferent woman with no understanding of a balanced diet. Her cooking was usually limited to fried foods. A pile of rat poison was on the floor next to the stove. Food had been placed in the refrigerator and forgotten. It decayed. Since the cook was also the housekeeper, the rectory was rarely cleaned. In the four years R. W. lived in the rectory, the windows in his room had been cleaned only once. R. W. left the ministry after finishing this assignment.

In some respects rectory living is like living in a military unit. One cannot pick where one lives or with whom one lives. Military commanders have learned, however, that the welfare of the troops requires that their quarters be clean and orderly and that healthy meals that are tastefully prepared be provided. Those involved in pastoral ministry deserve the same consideration.

Bishops have a clear responsibility to assure that when rectory living is required, the quarters are maintained in a satisfactory manner. Since a bishop has many other pressing duties, it is vitally important that pastors be selected with care. The practice of assigning a person as a pastor based on years of service alone does the Church a great disservice.

In summary, you will want to know well those people who work directly for you. You will need to be sensitive to their cares, concerns, and their financial needs. If you are responsible for the living conditions of others, you must provide clean, comfortable quarters and healthy, well-prepared meals. Your care and concern for staff members needs to permeate all levels of the organization.

Keep Your Workers Informed

An organization that does not keep its workers informed unnecessarily operates in the realm of mystery. Mystery gives way to rumor. Consequently, the competent leader keeps his or her people informed.

Some organizations publish a house journal, bulletin, or memo for employees. This works well, provided the information is published on a timely basis.

Staff meetings are an excellent way to disseminate information. Staff members immediately then carry information back to their departments. This method of distribution, however, is only as good as the communication skills of those who relay the message.

Keeping people informed helps build a team spirit. It lets others feel that they are "in the know." Team spirit is a sign of positive leadership.

In summary, you will want to keep staff informed about matters that affect them personally as well as matters that affect the organization as a whole. In so doing, you will eliminate the brushfires that are started by rumors and false information, and you will foster a feeling of teamwork in your organization.

Set the Example

The leader, by necessity, stands in the spotlight. If employees are expected to be at work on time, so must the leader. If employees are expected to maintain a neat and clean standard of appearance, so must the leader. "Do as I say, not as I do," is a saying that reflects an attitude that can cause trouble for a leader.

- Mrs. S. A. was an assistant to the Chief Operations Officer of a church activity and was responsible for gathering time cards. She criticized an employee for not having deducted an hour from his time card when he had taken time off for personal business during the day. The employee pointed out that he habitually came to work early and worked beyond his quitting time. He pointed out, too, that he often worked on his days off without compensation. Then in a moment of rare candor, he asked Mrs. S. A. about the hour she began her workday. Taken by surprise, she admitted that she arrived sometimes at 9:00 and sometimes at 9:30. She was especially vulnerable to criticism of her own work habits by an employee who gave his time so generously.

• Brother Lucian taught religion in a Christian Brothers high school. At the beginning of each school year he stood in front of the school welcoming the students, looking most distinguished in his habit and wearing a neatly trimmed beard. A few weeks later the school published its annual dress code. One of the rules forbade male students from growing facial hair. Brother Lucian then shaved off his beard. The students were dismayed. He no longer looked distinguished! Students began a petition to allow their teacher to again grow his beard. It was, of course, a technique used each year by a master teacher to draw students into a spirited discussion of responsibility, rules, and setting examples.

A leader's appearance, conduct, language, and demeanor have an undeniable impact on those he or she must influence. Taken as a complete package, they amount to setting an example for others.

In summary, since "leadership, not drivership" is your goal, the example you set will be an important element in your success in leading others.

Ensure that Tasks Are Understood, Supervised, and Accomplished

The leader is the one with the vision. Others in the organization may be responsible for specific tasks, but it is the leader who determines what direction the organization will follow. The leader uses oral or written communications to assign a portion of the work to individuals or groups. This communication is the beginning of a three-step process of being sure that your instructions are understood, supervised, and accomplished.

All of us have had the experience of discovering that our communications are not always understood. You may have made arrangements to meet someone at a place and time that seemed very clear, only to discover that they waited at a different location.

Part of a leader's job is to make certain that the chances for misunderstanding are minimized. Task assignments must be presented as clearly as possible. Brief, concise instructions are generally better than lengthy, complex, and wordy ones. After assuring that the instruction is as clear as possible, the leader may ask the person to repeat the instructions as a communications check. The "I'm hearing you say . . ." technique can be effective if it is not excessive. In this way, any misunderstandings in communications can be corrected before a project gets started. The leader may also set the example by repeating what he or she understands others to be saying.

Misunderstandings sometimes take place when a person fails to understand that a task has been assigned to them. This may happen at staff meetings where a project is discussed at length, but no one leaves the meeting believing that they have the responsibility to get things done.

- The liturgy committee met to discuss preparations for Thanksgiving services. Everyone shared their ideas. It was decided that appropriate decorations for the church should be ordered from a florist. When Thanksgiving arrived there were no decorations in the church. No one had left the planning meeting with the feeling that they were responsible.

The next step the leader takes is assuring that the task is supervised. A capable leader will not assume that once a project is under way, all will go according to plan. Costly mistakes and wasted time can be eliminated by supervising the work or making spot-checks. It does not mean that you always should be looking over someone's shoulder, but it does mean showing an interest in what your employees are doing.

- A pastor asked his accountant to devise a new budget format for the monthly finance committee meeting. When the accountant submitted it, the pastor examined the document carefully.

He pointed out several areas of interest that had not been included. The final version gave the finance committee the data they needed.

The final step is to assure that the task is accomplished. The most effective means to do this is to set a "suspense date" for its completion. This date is then marked on the calendar so that the leader will not forget to assure that the project has been completed as planned. Many good projects "slip through the cracks" because no one did any follow-up.

- In the previous example, the pastor called the accountant, told him of the revisions needed, and asked to have the revised version on his desk by June 15. He allowed a buffer of several days prior to the committee meeting in establishing that date and entered the date on his calendar.

Establishing a time for people to demonstrate their accomplishments may make you feel uncomfortable at first. For this reason, the manner in which the target date is stated becomes important. "John, we need to have that revised budget format soon. I'd like to have it on my desk by June 15," need not sound dictatorial. Effective leaders do set goals and deadlines.

In summary, as a skilled leader, you must remember to assure that tasks are understood (including who is to do the task), supervised, and accomplished.

Train Your Staff as a Team

Work is much more satisfying when people work together as a team to accomplish an organization's goals. Just as a football team would not be effective if its members played as individuals on the field, so an organization is less effective if it lacks teamwork.

When members of a staff or committee work together as members of a team, they benefit from the sharing of ideas and a sense of being contributors in meaningful work. Teamwork requires that everyone develop good listening skills. Business expert Max DePree puts it this way: "In most vital organizations, there is a common bond of interdependence, mutual interest, interlocking contributions, and simple joy. Part of the art of leadership is to see that this common bond is maintained and strengthened, a task certainly requiring good communication."[1]

Professors Kouzes and Posner observe, "The more everyone in the organization feels a sense of power and influence, the greater the ownership and investment they feel in the success of their organization."[2] But it requires a special effort on the leader's part to make it possible for people to feel they are part of a team.

Teamwork can be developed by leaders who propose problems and then ask each member for their comments and solutions. If this is a new method for your group, you may have to encourage those who tend to be quiet to contribute to the discussion. Some excellent ideas may be buried under a blanket of shyness. Once a course of action is identified, roles can be assigned so that various people can participate in a group effort.

- The success of the Toyota Motor Company has been attributed in part to a management style calling for teamwork among its employees. The workers have a sense of ownership in the company. Oddly enough, it was an American, W. Edwards Deming, who developed in the 1950s the concept of "total quality management"—a team effort by all workers. He was unable to convince American auto manufacturers, so he took his theory to Japan, where it has proved to be an incredible success. One observer commented, "Strong, visible, participatory management that promotes teamwork, eliminates fear and includes regular opportunities for problem-centered interaction and follow-up can't help but improve performance."[3]

In summary, to attain the best results in your organization, train your staff to work as a team.

Develop a Sense of Responsibility among Your Workers

Closely related to the concept of training staff members as a team is the concept of developing a sense of responsibility among them. In fact, teamwork requires the sharing of a sense